Dates & Destiney

OrangeBooks Publication

1st Floor, Rajhans Arcade, Mall Road, Kohka, Bhilai, Chhattisgarh 490020

Website:**www.orangebooks.in**

© Copyright, 2023, Author

All rights reserved. No part of this book may be reproduced, stored in a retrieval system, or transmitted, in any form by any means, electronic, mechanical, magnetic, optical, chemical, manual, photocopying, recording or otherwise, without the prior written consent of its writer.

First Edition, 2023

Dates & Destiny

LEARN NUMEROLOGY SECRETS FOR HEALTHY, WEALTHY & HAPPY LIFE

ABHIJEET KHATI

OrangeBooks Publication
www.orangebooks.in

Writing this book and by blessings of GAJANAN MAHARAJ, "GANI GAN GANAT BOTE".

LEARN NUMEROLOGY SECREATS FOR HEALTHY, WEALTHY & HAPPY LIFE

Preface

From 1 to 9, numbers always inspire us. They are essential to our survival, whether they take the form of our name, house number, vehicle number, or most importantly, our date of birth. Just as fingerprints are unique, so too are DOBs, but some have common traits as well. By analyzing these numbers, we can gain insights into our own lives as well as the lives of others. Numerology is a fascinating and unique science that requires knowledge of vibrations in traits. Mobile numbers are a modern approach to numerology that also generates valuable inputs into our lives. I hope these books assist individuals in understanding numbers well and choosing professional consulting.

Acknowledgements

This book is dedicated to my Father who always inspires me to work with dedication and commitment. My Teacher, DR Rohit Gadkari inspired me to write this book; his teachings and way of motivation helped me to achieve this Goal. My Mentor Sunil pandey sir, Pankaj chouhan sir, Gautam Roy sir and his deep knowledge in numerology also helped me to work towards my book, and finally, my gratitude to Renu Kohli ji for the name suggestion & all student and fellow numerologist who worked towards the collection of various date of Birth for my research towards this goal.

About The Author

My name is ABHIJEET KHATI. I am based in Chattisgarh. I am qualified as a software engineer and have my PG in Marketing and sales. I have been very fascinated with astro science from a very young age; I personally visited various Astrologer and Hasth Rekha Visheshgya and understand the concepts. But my journey started when I got in touch with numerology and found it very fascinating and easy to understand and also found it interesting when got to know various celebrities or corporate companies using these amazing helping science called numerology. I personally learned from various teachers and finally decided to compile all my learnings and my clients' experience to form a book. This is how my journey started.

Content

What Is Numerology 1

Number Traits 2

What Is Lo Shu Grid? 4

Details, Charaterstics Of Numbers 26

Basic Number (Molank) & Destiny (Bagyank) No 28

Lucky Numbers & Anti Numbers 36

Name Numbers 47

Kua Number (Angel Number) 72

Vedic Numerology 78

Personal Year, Month & Date 90

Missing Number & Their Remedies, Number 1 & Health Issues 95

Mobile Numerology 102

Celebrity Grid Analysis 108

Vedic Remedy 129

Data Base Collection Of Famous Celebrity, Sportsperson, Businessmen. 132

What is Numerology

Numerology = (Numerus) + Logos (word, Thoughts and expression) + logy (logic or science)

Numerology is a science of numbers used in character analysis that answers the question, "Who am I?" using the number of names and the date of birth.

Numerology is a useful tool for gaining insight into your inner self, as well as your abilities, aspirations, and chances and obstacles in life. It provides career, romantic, and financial assistance. Numerology is a self-help method that can help you discover more about your inner self and genuine nature. There is proof that neurology was practiced 10,000 years ago in Egypt, Greece, China, and Rome.

Numerology strengthens the conviction that each person is given life voluntarily, at a specific moment and place, that will allow him to have a chance to turn around in consciousness. Numerology offers us the chance to become more conscious of our own abilities, talents, and chosen paths for using them.

Benefits of Numerology

Numerology is mostly used as a self-help tool; it can help you better comprehend nature and your inner self.

- It presents facets of your character and personality in a novel and motivating way.

- It provides you with a fresh perspective on yourself that is more detached and forward-looking, and it gives you a better understanding of your advantages and disadvantages, which will benefit you in all facets of your life.

- Numerology also offers distinct perspectives on the chances and obstacles you have already encountered in other cycles. Numerology gives you a more positive outlook on life, helps you get ready for the future, and enables you to build on your advantages and conquer your disadvantages.

Number Traits

1. Independence, Freedom, Originality, Individualization, Attainment, Leadership, Beginnings, Innovator.

2. Corporation balance diplomacy the peacemaker, emotion, art, Peace, Literature, Poetry, Cooking, Domestic.

3. Self Expression, Growth, Creativity, Vision, Artistic, Wisdom, Social, Education, Knowledge, Spirituality, Purity.

4. System, Order, Limitations, Service, Practical, Foundations, Discipline, Revolution, Organized, Reliable, Systematic.

5. Variety, Constructive, Freedom, Change, Versatile, Explorer, Travel, Sensual, Materialistic, Adaptable, Finance, Speech, Communication, Trade.

6. Home and family, Beauty, Sensuality, Materialistic, Responsibility, Balance, Love, Caring, Protective, Nurturing, Community Oriented.

7. Analysis, Understanding, Knowledge, Wisdom, Introspective, Analytical, Spiritual, Research, Imagination.

8. Material Satisfaction, Authority, Power, Ambition, Giving and Receiving, Struggle, Hard work.

9. Humanitarianism, Selflessness, Idealist, Compassion, Completion, Universal Love, Anger, Energy, Activity.

There are Mainly 5 types of Numerology

Kabbalah Numerology - Hebrew Mysticism outgrowth of the Hebrew alphabet with its 22 vibrations. Later, it was adapted for the Greek alphabet and Roman alphabet. The 13th-century Kabbalists believed that the old Bible was written in secret code inspired by god. They used numerology as a tool to decipher the code.

Chaldean Numerology - This numerology originated with astrological originated Mesopotamia, which is also considered as birth place of western astrology. Each letter has a unique vibration and unique vibratuion and is assigned a number from 1 to 8 based on energetic equality. The number 9 is not included as it is considered as a sacred number. Single digits reveal the outer nature of person while double digits inner qualities.

Pythagorian - Developed by a Greek philosopher, Mathematician and Metaphysician of 6th Century BC. Numbers are assigned to the letters in Greek alphabets based on their position in Sequence. It uses both name and date of Birth and Examines relationships.

3	6	9
2	5	8
1	4	7

Chinese Numerology - Loshu Grid-Marking on turtle-shell Perfect Square with nine equal parts, Sum of all rows, Columns and Diagonal is 15.

4	9	2
3	5	7
8	1	6

Vedic Numerology - Vedic Numerology gives a very precise interpretation of future possibilities; it is mostly associated with the planetsand their simple calculation using various Dashas, Yearly Antar Dasha, Monthly Dashas and some yogs to give accurate results.

3	1	9
6	7	5
2	8	4

What is Lo Shu Grid?

The magic square on the tortoise was called the Lo Shu grid. It was a perfect 3 by 3 magic square; every row horizontally, vertically and diagonally added up to 15 and single no 6.

The position for each number is given in below 9 square box.

Loshu Grid is also called Laxmi Yantra

Loshu grid has total of 8 Planes and 2 Forms, Vertical & Horizontal.

4 Wealth Money Fortune	9 Fame Name, Energy	2 Spouse Relationship Partnership
3 Wisdom Family Health	5 Balance Stability Energy	7 Creativity Children Project
8 Knowledge Education Motivation	1 Career Planning Success	6 Friends Travel Helping people

There are Mainly three planes in Loshu Grid, Horizontal, Diagonal, and Vertical, also named as

1. Mental
2. Emotional
3. Practical

Mental Plane

4	9	2

The Arrow of Intellect (Mental plane)

The arrow comprises numbers 4, 9 and 2 in the first horizontal row. The presence of these three numbers gives intellectual ability and an excellent memory. This arrow belongs to people who are analytical, articulate and logical but who sometimes consider themselves to be superior to others. ExDate of birth 9/12/1946.

Name - Sonia Gandhi

Famous - Indian Politician

Emotional Plane 3-5-7

The middle row is called the emotional plane. After all, the heart is in the body. This plane includes spirituality, intuition, feelings and emotions. Golden Heart people, Deseson from Heart. They are trustworthy, Cheated Easily, Number of Disappointment, Good Human beings. They can't deny anything. Marriage is a Question mark for them.

Ex-Anup Jalota

DOB-29/07/1953

Singer-

Mental Plane

3	5	7

Practical Plane 8-1-6

The bottom row is called the practical plane. This encompasses physical labor, the ability to be good with one's hands, and the ability to be practical in everyday life. They find Logic in everything, Don't Trust easily, Learn from self-experience, Financial management is good, Authoritative people, Material success, and Excellence in Business.

Ex-Mahatma Gandhi

Famous - Freedom Fighter

DOB-2/10/1869

8	1	6

Thought Plane 4-3-8

The vertical rows are also interpreted. The first of these numbers 4, 3 and 8 is the thought plane. This reveals the person's ability to come up with ideas, create things and carry them to fruition. Sharp Memory, Creativity, Strong Imagination Power, Logical in life, Political Row, Always think before making decisions, Cleverness, Analysis.

Example - Sheela Dixit

4		
3		
8		

Will Plane 9-5-1

The middle vertical row numbers 9, 5 and 1 is the will plane. This gives determination and persistence to succeed. Very Strong willpower, Humanitarian nature, Intellectual capabilities, Satisfied, Sure shot success, and they Bounce back easily.

Example - Virat Kohli

Famous - Cricketer

DOB-5/5/1988

	9	
	5	
	1	

Action Plane 2-7-6

The final vertical row numbers 2, 7 and 6 is the action plan. This shows the person's ability to put their thoughts into action. They can convert thoughts into action, Make fast decision, Physically active, Always ready to take challenges, Sports person, Believe in doing than thinking about results, and Very Energetic.

Example - Sachin Tendulkar

Famous - Cricketer

		2
		7
		6

The three vertical rows make a natural progression. First of all, the person has to come up with an idea (thought plane). He or she has to have determination and persistence (will plane), otherwise, the idea will never be acted upon. The decision is made at this stage. Finally, the person needs to be able to put the idea and the determination into action (action plane).

Now, first of all, we analyse the below arrows:

The Arrows of Strength

Determination

- Emotional Balance
- Spirituality
- Intellect
- Prosperity

Planner

- WillPower
- Action

The Arrow of Determination

This arrow is made up of the numbers 8, 5 and 2. People with this arrow are patient, persistent and determined. They are happy to bite their time until the moment is right, and then act. No matter what happens to them they never lose sight of their goals. Someone born on June 23, 1986 would have the error of determination.

		2
	5	
8		

The Arrow of Emotional Balance

This follows the path of the era of emotional balance in the chart and consists of numbers 4, 5 and 6. People with this are compassionate, caring people who often make a career out of helping others. They are sensitive and intuitive and have an uncanny ability to understand other people's needs. These people can appear to be shy particularly in the growing up years, as children, they are quiet and gentle. Somebody born on April 15th, 1966 would have the arrow of emotional balance.

4		
	5	
		6

The Arrow of Spirituality (Emotional Plane)

This is particularly interesting as it is made up of the numbers 3, 5 and 7. It occupies the central horizontal row. It emphasizes the feelings, emotions and spiritual aspects of the people who have it. It indicates a serious approach to life and an inner calm and serenity that seldom appear before middle age. A person born on March 17, 1953 would have the arrow of spirituality.

3	5	7

The Arrow of Intellect (Mental plane)

The arrow comprises numbers 4, 9 and 2 in the first horizontal row. The presence of these three numbers gives intellectual ability and an excellent memory. This arrow belongs to people who are analytical, articulate and logical but who sometimes consider themselves to be superior to others. Eg. date of birth 4/9/1992.

4	9	2

The Arrow of Prosperity (Physical or Practical plane)

This is in the bottom horizontal row and is made up of numbers, 8, 1 and 6. People with the arrow of prosperity excel in the business and the commercial world. They are interested in money for their own sake and are not usually interested in the higher values of life.

People who have the arrow of prosperity, but also have no numbers on the top horizontal row are cold, calculating and unfeeling. They achieve great material success but do so by ignoring the feelings and needs of others. A person born on June 18, 1974 would have the arrow of prosperity.

8	1	6

The Arrow of the Planner (Thought plane)

This consists of the numbers 8, 3 and 4 in the first vertical row. The basic meaning of this arrow of a planner is someone who is shrewd, cunning and not very ethical. Consequently, it is sometimes known, fairly or not, as the politicians' arrow. Somebody born on May 18, 1943 would have the arrow of the planner.

4		
3		
8		

The Arrow of Willpower (Will plane)

This consists of the numbers 1, 5 & 9. People with this arrow are stubborn, persistent and determined. They are inclined to be argumentative and have strong opinions on a variety of subjects. This arrow is regarded as a symbol of success because people with it steadily persist until they reach their ultimate goal. Someone with the birthday of September 15, 1955 would have the arrow of willpower.

	9	
	5	
	1	

The Arrow of Action (Action Plane)

The keyword for this arrow is action. It consists of the numbers 6, 7 and 2 in the last vertical row.

People with this arrow need to be busy and love physical activities. They enjoy exercising and participating in sports. They have tremendous reserves of energy and are happiest when expanding it on some physical challenge. A person born on 12 July, 1962 would have the arrow of action.

		2
		7
		6

Arrows or planes having Missing Numbers

If the plane has all 3 Numbers, Present arrow's strength is – 100%

If the plane has 2 Numbers, Present arrow's Strength is – 66%

If the plane has 1 Number, Present arrow's Strength is – 33%

Arrow with missing the entire Numbers, arrow's Strength – 0%

Now, we analyze the arrows of weakness -

Arrow of Weakness

- Frustration
- Suspicion
- Loneliness
- Apathy
- Confusion

- Losses
- Indecision
- Poor memory

The arrow frustration in the Western chart is an absence of the numbers 4, 5 and 6. In the East, it is a diagonal arrow created by the absence of the numbers 8, 5 and 2. This arrow indicates many setbacks and frustrations. In the East, it is regarded as a sign of consistent failure. People who have this arrow should try to learn from every experience and think carefully before acting.

The Arrow of Suspicion (absence of 4, 5, 6)

This is created by an absence of the numbers 4, 5 and 6. This arrow indicates that people are suspicious, cynical and moody. They are inclined to worry and dwell on the negative side of life. This arrow revealed a great person indicating someone who always lives in the shade and never comes out into the full light of day.

The Arrow of Loneliness (absence of 3, 5, 7)

This arrow consists of the absence of the numbers 3, 5 and 7 in the center horizontal row. This arrow denotes a lack of feelings. People with this are so intent on achieving their goals that they forget their friends and family and consequently lack joy, love and laughter in their lives. They usually suffer enormously from loneliness in their old age.

4	9	2
8	1	6

The Arrow of Apathy (absence of 2, 6, 7)

This arrow is created when the chart lacks the numbers 7, 2 and 6 in the last vertical row. People with the arrow of apathy lack motivation and fail to grasp opportunities even when really handed to them. These people are indecisive, frightened of taking risks and generally achieve only a fraction of what they could do if they applied themselves.

4	9	
3	5	
8	1	

The Arrow of Confusion (absence of 3, 4, 8)

This arrow is caused by a lack of the numbers 8, 3 and 4 in the chart. It occupies the left-hand vertical column. People with this arrow are not logical, methodical or organized. They live from day to day, seldom making long-term plans. When they do, they usually sabotage the plans before they bear fruit.

	9	2
	5	7
	1	6

The Arrow of Losses (absence of 2, 5, 8)

This arrow is created by an absence of the numbers 8, 1 and 6 in the bottom horizontal row. Consequently, nobody has had this Arrow in their charts for the last Thousand Years, but it will appear again in the 21st century. These people will try to make money by participating in get-rich-quick schemes. They will constantly fail in these, and will not realize until their middle-age. If they have put the same amount of effort into a single worthwhile goal, they would have achieved success.

4	9	
3		7
	1	6

The Arrow of Indecision (absence of 1, 5, 9)

This is created by the absence of the numbers 1, 5 and 9 in the center vertical row. No one has had this arrow for the last 1000 years, but we will start to see it in the 21st century.

People with this arrow have a desperate desire to be accepted and liked. Consequently, they can be easily led and swayed by others. They will find it extremely hard to stand up for what they believe in, as they want to please everyone and are unable to express views that other people might not accept.

4		2
3		7
8		6

The Arrow of Poor Memory (absence of 2, 4, 9)

The arrow is created by the absence of the numbers 4, 9 and 2 in the top horizontal row. This arrow will not be found until the 31st century. Everyone born in the last century has had a 9 in his or her chart and everyone born in the next 1000 years will have a 2.

People with this arrow start out in life with strong intellectual capability, that gradually weakens as the person matures. These people are also frequently overwhelmed by the vivid nature of their thoughts and can suffer from mental imbalance.

3	5	7
8	1	6

Small Arrows

Detail and Deceit (1, 3)

- Litigation (3, 9)
- Peace of Mind (7, 9)
- Science (1, 7)

These four small arrows are created by joining the four middle numbers of the outside horizontal and vertical rows. These are the small arrows joining the number 1 and 3, 3 and 9, 9 and 7, and 7 and 1.

The Arrow of Detail and Deceit (1, 3)

This is the row created when the chart contains both 1 and 3. People with this combination enjoy the details of things. In fact, if there is more than one of each number, the person is inclined to be a perfectionist. There is a negative side to the arrow, too. People with that are inclined to be dishonest when it suits them. They may lie about something or conceal the truth to protect themselves.

3		
	1	

The Arrow of Litigation (3, 9)

This arrow is created when the chart contains both the numbers, 3 and 9. People with this combination are inclined to argue and become involved in disputes of all kinds. If these get too serious, they have to be settled in a court of law; that is why this combination is known as the arrow of litigation.

	9	
3		

The Arrow of Peace of Mind (7, 9)

The arrow is created when the chart contains both 9 and 7. People with this combination are positively confident and have a strong faith. The logic of the 9 helps the spirituality of the 7 and vice versa. The people can rise to different situations with equanimity, confident that everything will work out for the best.

	9	7

The Arrow of Science (1, 7)

People with charts that contain the numbers 1 and 7 are interested in the mysteries of the world we live in. They enjoy searching for hidden truths and can become so involved with their studies that they get lost in the search. They are usually interested in the Science (frequently those that concern the oceans).

		7
	1	

The Five Elements In Chinese Astrology

There are five elements:

Wood, Fire, Earth, Metal and Water.

Everything in the world is made up of above elements. These elements can be both productive and destructive.

The productive cycle:

Water supports wood, Wood burns, creating fire; Fire leaves ash (earth), and from Earth, we get Metal; when Metal liquefies, we get water, and Water supports wood.

The destructive cycle is as below

Wood draws from earth, Earth pollutes water, Water stops fire, Fire melts metal, and Metal cuts wood.

Element :

Wood - Creativity

Fire - Enthusiasm, Excitement and Energy Earth - Stability and Patience Metal - Support.

Water – Planning and Communication.

Numbers & Their Importance (1 to 9)

1. Sun-King-Raja-Father
2. Moon–Mother
3. Jupiter–Guru
4. Rahu
5. Mercury
6. Venus
7. Ketu
8. Saturn
9. Mars

1. Sun - King - Raja - Father Number 1

Vibration - Positive, Leader, Pioneer, They need attention and appreciation, Good Communication, Aggression, they don't follow others, they like to give orders, they are very Courageous, Independent, King-type behaviour, Centre of attraction.

Negative - Ego, Rude, Dominant, Selfish, stubborn, ego, demanding, adamant.

Finance - After one age it's Good.

Health issues - Stomach, Back pain, Chest, Eye.

Relationship - Check ego for a better relationship.

Bill Gates, Elon Musk, Sunil Gavaskar, Lala Lajpat Rai.

2. Moon - Mother Number 2

Vibration - Good in managing others, Caring, Emotional, Lonely, Pushing in life, attractive, Peaceful, Gentle, Sensitive, Creative, Intuitive, Instable, Family oriented; they can attract masses easily, they don't deny to anyone easily, they connect very easily, they want more love and support.

Negative - Easily get hurt, Mood swing.

Finance - Good money rotation but difficult for savings.

Health - Cold & cough, anxiety, mind-related issues.

Relationship - They take care of partners and family very well.

Rahul Dravid, Anu Kapoor, Kirti Azad, Sharukh Khan, Kapil Sharma.

3. Jupiter-Guru Number 3

Vibration - Knowledge, Spiritual, Family first, Earning sources are ready, Good Moral values, Teacher, Healer, Counsellor, They attract right guru easily, Social animal, Intellectual, Ready to learn always.

Negative - Over trust, they get diverted easily, sacrificing, taking too many tasks at one time, ignoring their own family, Procrastination.

Finance - Good Health, Skin and Stomach.

Relationship - Very responsible for taking care of family.

Ajay Maken, Rohit Sharma, Priya Darshan, Jaswant Singh.

4. Rahu Number 4-

Characteristic Rahu - Dabang

Vibration - Unpredictable, Double Minded, Electronic Non-Operational, Good Sharp mind, Good Memory, Good Observation, Convincing Skill Expenses, Practical, Disciplined, Fundamentalist.

Negative - Stubborn, adamant, argumentative, lack of imagination, experience bed health.

Finance - Money comes with a lot of hard work, Health - Gastric, Stomach, Chronic disease.

Relationship - Responsible, but lacking flexibility, Many times struggle in relationships.

Aditya Pancholi, Gurudass Mann, Varun Gandhi, Satish Kaushik, Amrish Puri.

5. Mercury Number 5

Characteristic 5 - Mercury

Vibration - Flexible, Communication, Business, Jugadu, Calculative, Money minded, Highly balanced, Social, Freedom lover, Sometimes lazy, Good in getting good opportunity, liquidity of money, Always a kind-hearted, Friendly. They can't focus on one work.

Finance - Money is good, but saving money is not there, come fast and go fast most of the times.

Health - SKIN, Stomach, Mind related.

Mark Juckerburg, Deepika Padukone, Sania Mirza, Aamir Khan, Shekhar Suman.

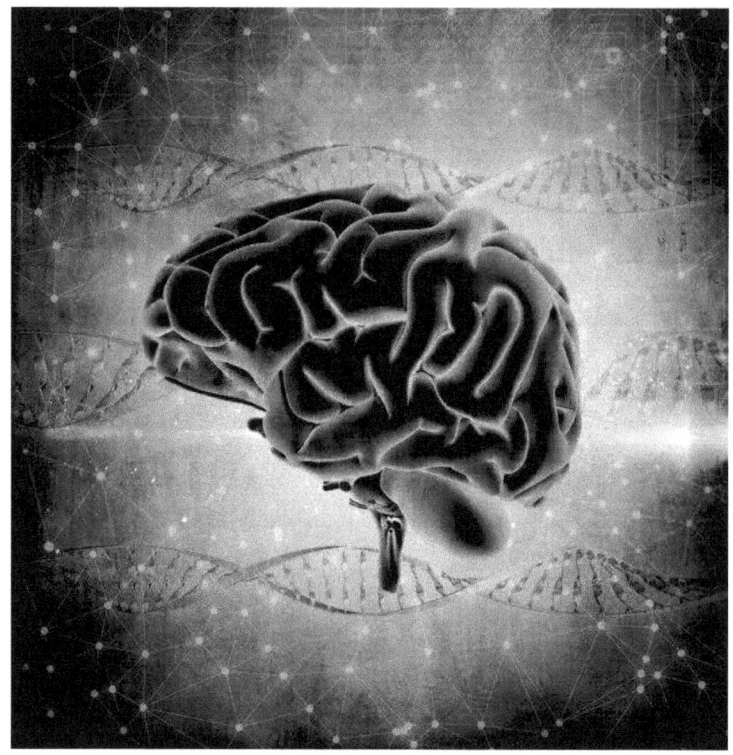

6. Venus Number 6

Characteristic 6 - Venus

Vibration - Luxury, Hard work, Friend circle, Good food, Comfort, Cleanness, Materialistic pleasure, Very good aura, Creative people, Love, Romance, Luxury, Responsible, Helping nature, Artistic, Media glamour, Jugadu person, Tit for tat, Singing, Music, Negative- Manipulative, Commitment not fulfilled, Cheat in multiple (Multiple 6).

Finance - Good

Health - Lower part of the body

Relationship - Good, Responsible, Don't like to stay alone.

Kapil Dev, W Saha, Alia Bhat, Subhash Ghai, Imran Hashmi, Ravindra Jadeja

7. Ketu Number 7

Characteristic 7 - Ketu Vibration - Loyalty, Stable, Family Support, Luck, Spiritual, They people settle in out of birth place, Truth seeker, Curious, Critical thinker, Good in studies, Research oriented, Deep dive, Straight forward, Secretive.

Negative - Health issues, they miss fun most of the time due to work Finance - it's Ok, earn from their skills.

Health - Cold & cough, skin related, lung problem.

Relationship - they don't open up much, mysterious.

Kabir Bedi, Shahid Kapoor, Wasim Zafar, Rajpal Yadav, Karan Johar.

8. Saturn Number 8

Characteristic 8 - Saturn Vibration - Hard work, Depression, You have to work very hard to get success, Delay, Money loss, Instability, Efforts, Struggle, Logical, Powerful.

Negative - Stubborn, everything with struggle.

Finance - After 38 years, they have good money.

Health - Sinus, Chronic disease, Relationship - They are dedicated lover & protective.

Ravi Teja, Javeed Akhtar, Anil Kumble, R Ashwin.

9. Mars Number 9

Characteristic 9 - Mars

Vibration - Bold, Aggressive, Angry, Memory Average, Action, Good Human being, Spiritual, They are pet lovers, Healing professionals.

Negative - Ego, Unpredictable, impulsive, Moody, Success delay.

Finance – Good, Health - Stomach, Digestion, Accident, Relationship - Ok, they want an adjusting partner.

Farhan Akhtar, Shahi Kapoor, Salman Khan, Shashi Tharoor.

Details, Charaterstics Of Numbers

No.	Date Of Birth	Ruling Planet	Personality	Characterstics				
1	1,10,19,28	Sun	King	Leader				
2	2,11,20,29	Moon	Queen	Intutive				
3	3,12,21,30	Jupiter	Teachears	Wisdom				
4	4,13,22,31	Rahu	Mysterious	Disciplined				
5	5,14,23	Mercury	Prince	Communication				
6	6,15,24	Venus	Devil Teachear	Charming				
7	7,16,25	Neptune (Ketu)	Disciples	Spiritual				
8	8,17,26	Saturn	Judge	Laborious				
9	9,18,27	Mars	Commander	Kind Hearted				Commander

8 Planes Of Numero Kundali (3 Horizontal, 3vertical & 2 Diagonal Plans)

EMOTIONAL PLAN — row 3,5,7

MEMORY PLAN — row 4,9,2

PRACTICAL PLAN — row 8,1,6

THOUGHT PLAN — column 4,3,8

WILL POWER PLAN — column 9,5,1

ACTION PLAN — column 2,7,6

SUCCESSFUL PLAN 1 — diagonal 4,5,6

SUCCESSFUL PLAN 2 — diagonal 2,5,8

Basic number (Molank) & Destiny (Bagyank) No

Your Inclination conduct and Character are directed by the Essential number and Destiny number. Fundamental number is dynamic in that it implies qualities of fundamental numbers are seen more between the age of 1-35 or till the time individual gets married. After 35 years, Fate number (Bag yank) takes over Destiny number more clarity of mind about a person's career, Cash Repayment or relationship with accomplice.

Your ongoing circumstance is an absolute choice you have taken up to this point, and your life will be full of consequences of the multitude of choices taken by you in your life. This generally relies upon their view of the situation, The discernment depends on their characteristic nature, This nature is the main driver and is characterized by DESTINY number.

Basic Numbers (Moolank)

The day of the month that you were born is also examined when we are doing any analysis in numerology. In calendars, each day has its own special quality or vibration.

The variation of the day of birth is as important as the destiny number. The day of the birth modifies the qualities of the destiny number, for example, people who have a 7 destiny number are likely to be quiet and introspective wherever they were born on the 3rd, 12th, 21st and 30th of the month. They would gain some of the outgoing expressive qualities of the three and would be much more communicative than most people with the 7 destiny number.

Moolank 2 At Your Best

Independent, Confident, Original, Strong, Action-Orientated, Capable, Positive, Goal-Oriented, Determined, Innovative, Creative, Problem-Solver, Fearless, Driven, Pioneer, Proactive, Uninhibited, Motivated, Freedom-Loving, Brave, Passionate, Resilient, Courageous, Resourceful, Persistent, Tenacious. Creative, Passionate, Generous, Warm-hearted, Cheerful, Humorous.

At Your Worst

Forceful, Domineering, Overly Ambitious, Reckless, Self-Doubt, Insecure, Fear of Failure, Sensitive to Criticism, Impatient, Short-Sighted, Self-Centred, Rebellious, Proud, Aggressive, Competitive, Stubborn, Know-It-All, Bossy, Directive, Isolated, Arrogant, Stubborn, Self-centered, Lazy, Inflexible.

Moolank 3 At Your Best Communicative, Creative, Artistic, Charming, Magnetic, Optimistic, Communicator, Zest for Life, Original, Curious, Fun, Engaging, Loving, Joyful, Enthusiastic, Light-Hearted, Jovial, Sociable, Optimistic, Youthful, Entertaining, Carefree, Uninhibited.

At Your Worst

Childish, Spoilt, Moody, Depressed, Naïve, Poor Judgement, Unfocused, Scattered, Shallow, Irresponsible, Emotional, Prideful, Selfish, Dramatic, Needy, Superficial, Narcissistic, Undisciplined.

Moolank 4 At Your Best

Strong, Stable, Organized, Service-Orientated, Poised, Dependable, Productive, Punctual, Trustworthy, Patient, Traditional, Reliable, Steady, Persistent, Humble, Down to Earth, Disciplined, Loyal, Dry Humour, Devoted, Consistent, Diligent, Patient, Enduring, Principled, Respected, Practical, Logical, Hardworking, Responsible, Resolute, Stable, Secure, Truthful, Honest, Constant, Wise, Rational.

At Your Worst

Solitary, Dispassionate, Territorial, Dogmatic, Conservative, Picky, Rigid, Inflexible, Workaholic, Controlling, Intolerant, Moralistic, Prejudiced, Strict, Stubborn, Slow, Tedious, Skeptical, Sullen, Risk-Adverse, Boring, Dull, Directive, Uncompromising.

Moolank 5 At Your Best

Vibrant, Freedom-Loving, Dynamic, Daring, Independent, Adventurous, Risk-Taker, Curious, Versatile, Adaptable, Quick Learner, Tolerant, Progressive, Sociable, Funny, Quick Witted, Resilient, Resourceful, Free-Thinker, Spontaneous, FreeSpirit, Charming, Unconventional, Eclectic, Outgoing, Experimental, Flexible, Energetic.

At Your Worst

Irresponsible, Careless, Unpredictable, Directionless, Selfish, Restless, Impulsive, Unreliable, Moody, Volatile, Excessively Sensual, Thoughtless, Indulgent, Fickle, Addicted, Rash, Easily Distracted, Non-Committal, Uncaring, Inconsistent.

Moolank 6 At Your Best

Loving, Caring, Healing, Protecting, Sympathetic, Fair, Just, Responsible, Graceful, Warm, Humorous, Respected, Dutiful, Harmonious, Romantic, Dedicated, Loyal, Honest, Humanitarian, Kind, Faithful, Compassionate, Understanding, Nurturing, Supportive, Empathetic, Sincere, Affectionate, Protective.

At Your Worst

Meddling, Intolerant, Over-Involved, Self-Sacrificing, Intrusive, Jealous, Small Minded, Smug, Arrogant, Self-Righteous, Zealot, Obsessive, Anxious, Self-Centered, Egotistical, Cynical, Merciless, Martyr, Domineering, Controlling, Poor Judgement of Character, Idealistic.

Moolank 7 At Your Best

Intellectual, Philosophical, Curious, Wise, Smart, Visionary, Seeker, Mystic, Curious, Eccentric, Spiritual, Intuitive, Deep, Inquisitive, Analytical, Introspective, Perceptive, Mysterious, Mental Explorer.

At Your Worst

Cold, Aloof, Cynical, Arrogant, Oblivious, Untruthful, Judgmental, Uncaring, Unsociable, Perfectionist, Reclusive, Demanding, Odd, Secretive, Suspicious, Reserved, Solitary, Sceptical, Silent.

Moolank 8 at Your Best

Successful, Driven, Ambitious, Courageous, Goal-Orientated, Practical, Rational, Intelligent, Generous, Spiritual, Efficient, Disciplined, Focused, Astute, Considered, Powerful, Prosperous, Motivated, Self-Confident, Honest, Forgiving, Tenacious, Reliable, Professional, Resourceful, Solution-Focused, Karmic, Enduring.

At Your Worst

Materialistic, Arrogant, Authoritarian, Angry, Frustrated, Aggressive, Dissatisfied, Greedy, Intolerant, Entitled, Hating, Dominant, Haughty, Prideful, Abusive, Intolerant, Reckless.

Moolank 9

At Your Best

Wise, Experienced, Spiritual, Humanitarian, Aware, Worldly, Sophisticated, Loving, Compassionate, Non-Judgemental, Tolerant, Conscious, Communicative, Giving, Charming, Engaging, Confident, Generous, Creative, Patient, Kind, Understanding, Intuitive, Aware, Tolerant.

At Your Worst

Cold, Arrogant, Condescending, Cruel, Egotistical, Resentful, Sacrificing, Aloof, Removed, Unavailable.

Destiny Numbers

We start our investigation by working out a destiny number. This is by and largely viewed just like the main number in Chinese number sensitivity, yet it uncovers a reason throughout everyday life. A great many people have little thought of how they ought to do their lives, and information on this number all alone can change their lives.

There are 12 potential destiny numbers 1, 2, 3, 4, 5, 6, 7, 8, 9, 11, 22 and 33. 11, 22 & 33 are called the Expert Numbers and contain more power than different numbers.

We decide our destiny number by including the digits of our date of birth and lessening the response to a solitary digit. If you lessen the numbers, the complete comes to 11, 22 or 33; stop by then.

Destiny number is gotten from your birth dates. It is a significant illustration to be learnt in this life, the focal point of the individual's presence. Your destiny number is the street you are voyaging. It depicts the valuable open doors accessible to get familiar with the significant illustrations along with the climate where these open doors will be found.

This number is at the heart of the core. Visualize the life path as a broad channel for Highway running through all the possible activities a person may encounter in a lifetime. It is you what you are, really like what you are fitted to do.

Meaning of the Destiny Numbers

Each of the destiny numbers has a specific meaning. In this chapter, we will learn how the destiny number affects our life.

Destiny Number 1

People with Destiny number 1 have to learn to stand on their own feet and achieve something. They usually start out in life by being dependent and gradually achieve a degree of Independence as they mature. Ultimately, they often become pioneers, innovators and leaders.

One can be self-centered and like to be at the head of the line. Consequently, they are ambitious, progressive, determined and stubborn. They have inquiring minds and considerable leadership qualities. They have executive skills and can rise to the ranks of the ultimate opposition in their field. They have strong personal needs that need to be met. Although this may be disguised to others, people with Destiny number 1 are aware of it themselves. Whatever their needs are, one makes sure that they are met.

There is a negative side to Destiny Number 1. Someone finds it hard to achieve Independence and seem overly dependent. Consequently, they will be taken advantage of by others and will deeply resent it, even though they feel powerless to prevent it.

Another side to the Destiny Number 1 is that people try to build themselves up by pulling others down. They have ego problems and think of themselves first.

Destiny Number 2

People with Destiny number 2 are able to make people feel at ease. They are gracious and charming and make wonderful hosts and hostesses. They are sensitive to the needs of others and find it easy to make friends. They prefer being in a permanent relationship to being on their own. They are sensitive, peace-loving and have natural intuition. They can be good friends and express their feelings well. They are not overly concerned with the status of material needs. Consequently, they often find themselves in the number 2 position rather than the number 1. They are content to be the power behind The Throne. In this position, they do not always receive the full recognition that they should, but they are usually content knowing that they have done a good job.

Occasionally, you will find people with Destiny Number 2 who are using their skills negatively. They will try desperately to become leaders, preferring to be mediocre in this role instead of outstanding in the number 2 position. Although they may achieve their aims, they will never feel comfortable or happy in a leadership role.

Destiny Number 3

People with Destiny Number 3 need to express themselves in some sort of way ideally creative. As this expression usually uses verbal skills, it can include singing, talking and writing. Threes usually have excellent conversation and enjoy expressing all the joys of life. Communication is their forte. They have active imaginative brains and are always full of ideas. However, they often lack the motivation to put them into play. People with this Destiny Number are friendly, sociable and outgoing. They enjoy having others around them and cannot stand being on their own for very long. People with this Destiny Number are soft-hearted and less-attached to the materialistic world.

Some people with Destiny Number 3 use it negatively by being superficial and scatter-brained. They dabble in numerous areas but never take anything very far. Lack of purpose leads to over-indulging in alcohol drugs and/or sex.

Destiny Number 4

People with Destiny Number 4 need to work hard to achieve their goals. They are practical, reliable, conscientious and well-organized people who enjoy keeping to routines. They are able to create order out of chaos. They are hard workers who enjoy seeing the result of their labor. Fours are prepared to patiently plod along for years provided they can see that the effort is worthwhile. They are good with details and enjoy fine complicated tasks. Inclined to being rigid and stubborn, they find it very hard to change their minds once it has been made up. They have strong likes and dislikes and are not afraid to express their views.

Many people with Destiny 4 use their skills negatively. These people dislike their feelings of limitations and destruction and try to find them by becoming dominating and abusive.

Destiny Number 5

People with Destiny Number 5 are versatile and enjoy doing a wide variety of different things. Feel restless and impatient when they feel restricted in any way. They enjoy travel excitement and anything that takes them out of their familiar routines. They are quick thinkers who enjoy solving problems. Early on in life, they are inclined to dabble, but once they find their correct path, they frequently achieve a great deal. These people are always curious, enthusiastic and forever young at heart.

Negative side of Destiny Number 5 is over-indulgence. These people often change elections and find it impossible to stick to anything for long. Many experiments with and over-indulge in alcohol, drugs and sex.

Destiny Number 6

People with Destiny Number 6 are nurturing, caring and responsible. They enjoy accepting other people's burdens and providing a shoulder for others to lean on. They particularly enjoy helping the people they care for. They become the member of the family that the other turns to when things are not going well. Sixes are capable of solving problems between others in such a way that everyone feels happy with the outcome. Sympathetic, loving and kind, they are happiest when surrounded by their friends and loved ones. Sixes are often creative, usually in artistic fields.

It is rare to find people with Destiny Number 6 using their skills negatively. However, sixes who accept everyone's responsibilities often end up being overwhelmed by everyone else's problems.

Destiny Number 7

People with Destiny Number 7 need time by themselves to grow in knowledge and wisdom. They have their own special unique approach to everything they do. This gives them great originality but also means that they find it hard to make changes and adapt. It also can sometimes make it difficult for them to feel comfortable as a part of a group.

Sevens prefer a few close friends to large groups of acquaintances. They can be hard to get to know initially, as they protect themselves with their barriers, but they make good friends once they fully trust the other person. Reserved, cautious and introspective, sevens are spiritual. People and their philosophy of life grow and develop as they go through life.

People on the negative side find it impossible to get close to others and hide themselves away. They become increasingly introspective and self-centered.

Destiny Number 8

People with Destiny Number 8 enjoy being involved in large-scale enterprises and want to reap the reward of their success. They set worthwhile goals for themselves and then go out and achieve their goals. They are ambitious and determined and invariably achieve their aims. Eights live very much in the real world and have no time, Dreamers. They are good at dealing with money, and once they achieve their financial goals, they can be very generous. They are good judges of character. They have leadership capabilities and usually rise to positions of responsibility. Eights are inclined to be rigid and stubborn in outlook, so usually, they cannot see this trait in themselves.

People, who use their skills negatively, achieve large sums of money but do so at the cost of health, happiness and relationships. They can become intolerant, vengeful and power-hungry.

Destiny Number 9

People with the Destiny Number 9 are inclined to be self-sacrificing, sensitive, caring people with a strong need to serve others. They will enjoy helping others and frequently give much more than they receive and return. Consequently, they can easily be taken advantage of by others. Nines are romantic, soft-heated and are profoundly disappointed when their deep true love is not returned. These humanitarian aims of the nines are usually slightly detached and universal in scope. Nine is the third creative number, and these people often express their creativity in writing, so it can come out in many different ways.

You will find many negative people having Destiny Number 9. This is because, it is so difficult to remain selfless. They never find any satisfaction in this, as they are fighting their true nature.

Lucky Numbers & Anti Numbers

Luck numbers are those having equal energy wave length, or having similar elements matching.

Anti-numbers are those having different or opposite wave lengths.

Neutral numbers are those that either be a friend or are kept in enemy.

Number	Represent	Anti	Lucky
1	Sun	8	9, 2, 5 & 3
2	Moon	4, 8, 9, 6	1, 5, 3
3	Jupiter	6	1, 5, 2
4	Rahu	9, 2, 4, 8	7, 6, 1, 5
5	Mercury	NA	1, 2, 3, 6
6	Venus	3, 9, 2	1, 4, 5, 7
7	Ketu	NA	1, 3, 4, 5, 6
8	Saturn	1, 2, 4, 8, 9	3, 6, 7
9	Mars	2, 4, 6, 8	1, 3, 5

Repeated impact in Lo-Shu

Numbers & their Grid– Multiple 1

Every Date of birth is comprised of various numbers and these numbers also show results based on vibrations of numbers and how many numbers repeat in the date of birth, Some show great results and sometimes give negative energy as well. Please find number 1 to 9, and their intensity as per numerology chart calculation.

Single 1 - They can't express their innermost thoughts, they can have difficulties to understand the outer world people.

Double 1 - They can communicate well, able to understand other people.

1. 111 - They are like a chatter box. Many times, silent and uncommunicative; they are a good planner.

2. 1111 - Can't Express, very sensitive, compassionate, sometimes, create misunderstanding, it's difficult for them to relax, they are hyper most of the time.

3. 11111 - They are least likely to be comfortable giving speeches to large audiences. They are good in creativity- writer, dancer. Tendency to overindulge in food, wine and love.

Repeated impact in Lo-Shu
Numbers & their Grid– Multiple 2

Single 2 - They are sensitive and can easily have their feelings hurt, they are fast to recognize people.

1. 2 & 2 - They are bright and intuitive, which make them excellent psychics.

2. 2-2-2 - They are more sensitive and have a tendency to withdraw, focus issue at work, dual-minded working at the same time.

3. 2222 - They might be challenging to deal with since they are impatient, people find them strange, therefore, they are alone.

4. 22222 - They are born complainers/fake.

Repeated impact in Lo-Shu
Numbers & their Grid– Multiple 3

Single 3 - They have an excellent memory and a clear view of their goal; they are positive and natural leaders with good moral values.

1. 3-3 - They are highly creative and are able to express their felling very well, less of moral values.

2. 333 - Extremely imaginative, living in their own universe, making it difficult for them to relate with outer world at times, a day dreamer.

3. 3333 - They may appear as if they are their world, but they think people trying to harm them, over imaginative.

Repeated impact in Lo-Shu
Numbers & their Grid– Multiple 4

Single 4 - They are very neat and tidy in their appearance and surroundings; they are involves in work that is systematic in nature.

1. 44 - They are highly materialistic; they enjoy their work, incredibly artistic and creative.

2. 444 - They are athletic and hard-working, yet they spend majority of their time doing the wrong work or practising.

3. 4444 - They excel at job that require them to use their hand, lots of effort and select career that require physical labour.

Repeated impact in Lo-Shu
Numbers & their Grid– Multiple 5

Single 5 - Wants lots of freedom in relationships and work, one can't tie them down, very caring and well-balanced, constructive in their approaches, good at motivating others.

1. 5-5 - They are determined and hardworking, sometimes lazy, money-minded but don't ask for money to anyone.

2. 555 - Compulsive talkers, don't think before speaking, they are daring and travel to different places.

3. 5555 - They get prone to accidents or also cause one itself, become impulsive and don't think through before acting.

Repeated impact in Lo-Shu
Numbers & their Grid– Multiple 6

Single 6 - They are very close to their family and like to maintain pleasant surroundings, good listeners and advisors, and most of the time, people ask for their advices.

1. 6-6 – Very creative but also dominating, very large friend circle, instability in relationship, Harsh speech.

2. 666 - Having a bad temper, they should learn to control it, they excel in their chosen industry as a result, and their creativity must be channelled.

3. 6666 - They are misfit as a child, as they are highly emotional and creative, can be fraud many times, associates with disputes and controversies.

Repeated impact in Lo-Shu
Numbers & their Grid– Multiple 7

Single 7 - They shall have a lesson by losing something close to them might a person or object, travel more, and the Luck factor is more.

1. 77 - They are interested in the spiritual world and life, health can be an issue, No stability in life, meaningful travels.

2. 777 - They lead unfortunate lives, they can be cheated very easily, financial losses.

3. 7777 - Suspicious, secretive, Health issues and finances.

Repeated impact in Lo-Shu
Numbers & their Grid– Multiple 8

Single 8 - Constructive, they have busy minds, and enjoy a wide range of experience. They don't like to do routine jobs.

1. 88 - They are sharp and thoughtful, they prefer to take action rather than sit and listen. They stick to their decision after made them, good money after one age.

2. 888 - Extremely helpful, relationship issues at an early age, delay in marriage; they are materialistic, they are great business people, they want all great comforts for themselves.

3. 8888 - They are restless, always looking for something new, either they travel a lot, or they can have litigation issues.

Repeated impact in Lo-Shu
Numbers & their Grid– Multiple 9

Single 9 - Intelligent enough to distinguish between good and bad, they are very good learners, aggressive.

1. 99 - They think they are very intelligent, self-esteem is very high, aggressive and have a lots of jobs, very good human beings.

2. 999 - He is a person with a very high energy or aggression or angry; they can go into technical or police, army, as they are very impulsive.

3. 9999 - They are extremely intelligent, live in their own world; if energy and intelligence are channelized properly, they can have a good impact on society and become great leaders.

D -C	Driver & conductor no combination with effects
1-4, 4-1	Sometimes king, sometimes beggar.
1-8, 8-1	Up down in career, Egoless, Bad relation with father Problem government work, Accident, family problems.
1-9, 9-1	Canbeengineer, doctor or any other good position, courageous and successful, freely doing his work without any support.
2-4, 4-2	Marriage problems; (female) health problems, Mood swings, Confusion, Family tension and Low concentration, Result only after Hard work.
2-6, 6-2	Extra marital affair, diabetes chance, urinary problem, divorce chance.
2-8, 8-2	Emotional pain, tension, hurdles in life, much work and less result, very bad combination, depression, negative thoughts, problems, bad relation with mother, always in some fear. Good for financial stability after 40 years.
2-9, 9-2	Marriage problem.
3-6, 6-3	Professionally very good but marriage disturbs (male only).
3-7, 7-3	High education, might become Govt official, high post all because of Good studies.
4-4	Professional struggle no settlement.
4-8, 8-4	Professional struggle, Late success, negative thoughts, fear, fertility problem, good for government work or success.
4-9, 9-4	Health problems (always hit health) and operation chance.
5-8, 8-5	Property
6-6	Additional marital affairs before and after marriage.
6-9, 9-6	Controversies in life always, Multiple relationships, delayed marriage, good for financial success, hard worker.
7-7	Health disturbed, Fraud and loss.
8-9, 9-8	Health and professional struggle.
9-9	Late Marriage, married life disturbed Born intelligent.

81 Combinations

These Combinations are based upon your Driver Number and Conductor number which is the sum total of your date of birth, for example, 3/12/1982 of driver number 3 and sum total is 8, so as per their energy, we interpret their compatibility. Please find attached 9*9, equal to 81 combination.

1-1 Average	2-1 VG	3-1 VG	4-1 Average	5-1 VG	6-1 Average	7-1 VG	8-1 VB	9-1 VG
1-2 Average	2-2 Average	3-2 Average	4-2 Bad	5-2 Average	6-2 Bad	7-2 Average	8-2 VB	9-2 Average
1-3 VG	2-3 Average	3-3 Average	4-3 Good	5-3 Average	6-3 Bad	7-3 VG	8-3 Average	9-3 VG
1-4 Average	2-4 Bad	3-4 Good	4-4 Bad	5-4 Good	6-4 Good	7-4 Good	8-4 VB	9-4 VB
1-5 VG	2-5 Average	3-5 Average	4-5 Good	5-5 Average	6-5 Good	7-5 Average	8-5 VG	9-5 Average
1-6 Average	2-6 Bad	3-6 Bad	4-6 Good	5-6 Good	6-6 Average	7-6 Average	8-6 Good	9-6 VB
1-7 VG	2-7 Average	3-7 VG	4-7 Good	5-7 Average	6-7 Average	7-7 Bad	8-7 Average	9-7 Average
1-8 VB	2-8 VB	3-8 Average	4-8 VB	5-8 VG	6-8 Good	7-8 Average	8-8 Bad	9-8 Average
1-9 VG	2-9 Bad	3-9 VG	4-9 VB	5-9 Average	6-9 VB	7-9 Average	8-9 Average	9-9 Average

VG=Very good

VB= Very bad

Name Numerology

Chaldean Numerology

In the Chaldean Numerology System, each alphabet is assigned a number from 1 to 8. The number is calculated using the values assigned to each alphabet we calculate the sum of numbers and find a single number called name number.

A number is always unique to an individual a either rich person a company's name or a famous sports person, a name vibration always surrounds them, so a correct name synchronizes with Destiny Number gives superb results. Celebrities and sports people also impacted their celebrity status after changing name vibration, Bollywood movie name created humongous results after the name change.

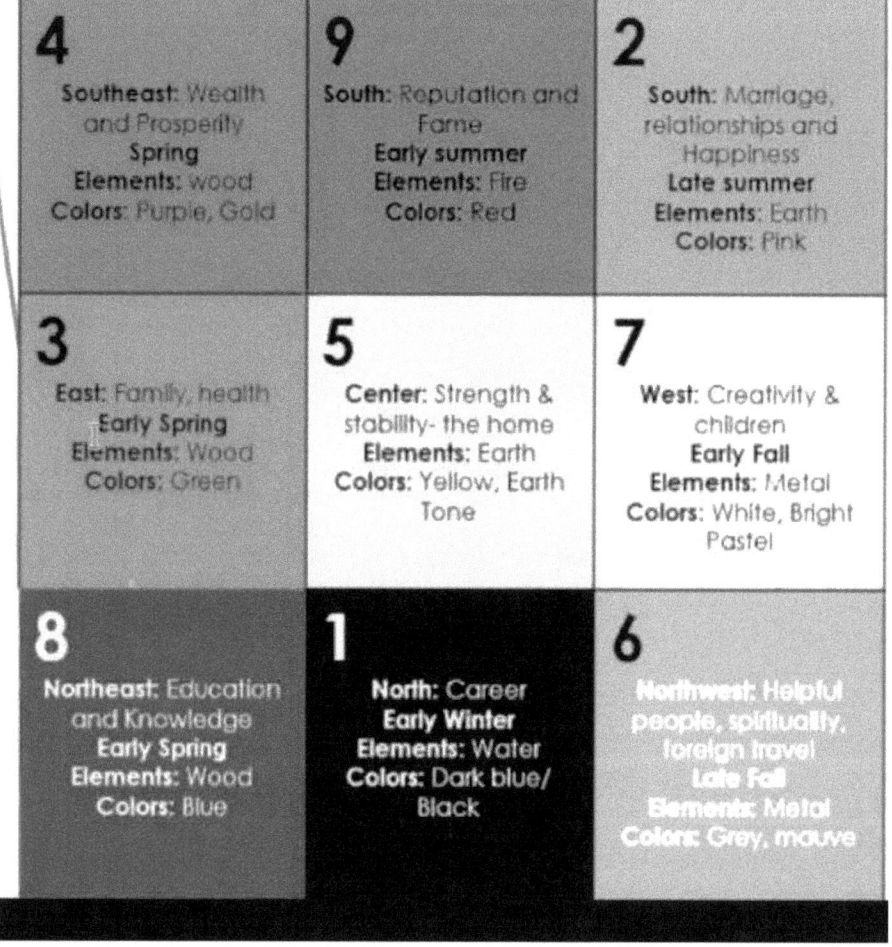

1	2	3	4	5	6	7	8
A	B	C	D	E	U	O	F
I	K	G	M	H	V	Z	P
J	R	L	T	N	W		
Q		S		X			
Y							

Numro value to alphabet (A to Z)

Example - RAM AHUJA 7+5=12

R=2+A=1+M=4 =7

A=1+H=5+U=6+ J=1+ A=14

(AHUJA=1+4=5)

| Ram 7 | Ahuja 5 | Ram Ahuja 7+5=12 | Total 1+2=3 |

As per lo shu grid RAM AHUJA DOB 24/11/1993

4	99	2
3, 3C, 3N		
	1,1,1	6D

C - Condustor number, D - Driver number, N - Name number

Driver number is 6 and Destiny number is 3, since there is an enemy combination, so the Name number should not be with number 3, as per Loshu Grid Analysis.

Missing numbera are 5 and 8, and number 3 is also coming 3 times, so better to change name number to 5.

So, the new name no is RRAM AHUJA

      2214   15611

Compound /name total is 23=5

Chaldean Name Numerology Reading Of Rram Ahuja

Rram Ahuja
2214 15611

Compound Name Number/Namank (Numerology Total of Your Name): **23**

Famous Celebrity Name Change

CELEBRITY NAME	NAME AFTER CHANGE	DATE OF BIRTH
AYUSHMAN KHURANA-TOTAL NO 3	AYUSHMANN KHURRANA-TOTAL NAME NO 1	14/9/1984
TUSHAR KAPOOR-TOTAL NAME NO 3	TUSHAR KAPOOR-TOTAL NAME NO 6	20/11/1976
AJAY DEVGAN-TOTAL NO 1	AJAY DEVGAN -TOTAL NAME NO 9	2/4/1969
SUNIL SHETTY-TOTAL NO 4	SUNIL SHETTY-TOTAL NAME NO 9	11/08/1961
RAJKUMMAR RAO -TOTAL NAME NO 5	RAJKUMMAR RAO- TOTAL NAME NO 6	31/08/1984
KARISHMA KAPOOR-TOTAL NAME NO 1	KARISHMA KAPOOR-TOTAL NAME NO 6	25/06/1974
RANI MUKHERJI-TOTAL 8	RANI MUKHERJI -TOTAL NAME NO 3	21/03/1978
HRITHIK ROSHAN-TOTAL 2	HRITHIK ROSHAN-TOTAL 7	10/01/1974
VIVEK OBEROI-TOTAL NAME NO 8	VIVEK OBEROI-TOTAL NO 9	3/9/1976
JAVED JAFFREY-TOTAL NAME NO 8	JAVED JAFFREY-TOTAL NO 9	4/12/1963

Companies And There Name Number

COMPANY NAME	NAME NUMBER
GOOGLE	TOTAL 28=1
MICROSOFT	TOTAL 39=12=3
APPLE	TOTAL 25=7
TATA	TOTAL 10=1
RELIANCE	TOTAL 25=7
ADANI	TOTAL 12=3
NOKIA	TOTAL 25=7
CANON	TOTAL 25=7
BMW	TOTAL 12=3
MARUTI	TOTAL 18=9

Name Numbers

1. Communication (Verbal)
2. Intuition Power, Sensitivity
3. Imagination Power
4. Discipline, Organized
5. Balance Emotion
6. Home & Family
7. Research & Disappointments
8. Struggle, Discipline, Organized
9. Humanitarian

Name Numbers

Name Numerology:

Name numerology is the main part of Chaldean Numerology:

Name numbers 1 and 2 are impossible for anyone, so we will start Name number from 3 and will see up to 100.

Name number 3:

Wisdom

- Happy and Jolly person, Knowledge lover, Divine interest.
- Loves reading books, Good in academics.
- Go up in life because of their personal efforts.
- They progress in life stage by stage, and ultimately, reach great heights.
- Are honest persons. Good number.

Name number 4:

- Can take wrong ways, Unnecessary waste of resources and wealth.
- Subject themselves to the authority of others, You take knowledge of many things, so not useful, Not a good name, need correction.
- Up down in your life. Struggle and delay.
- Avoid this name number for overall success.

Name number 5:

- Have multitalented, Multiple sources of income.
- Money-minded, Very practical
- Loves freedom, They are full of self-confidence and firmness Want to enjoy life like travelling, movie, disco etc., A good number, They enjoy the bliss of divine grace.
- They like the modern, They invent new things.

Name number 6:

- Loving, caring, sweet and peaceful person, Want material success and accumulation. Attract masses, They are calm by temperament.
- Love art of every form.
- Good number.

Name number 7:

- They have any layers in their personality.
- Very secretive, Seeker of wisdom.
- Always search for deeper meaning.
- Smart and learned but don't deserve success.
- It brings the grace of the divine, There is no pleasure in family life.

Name number 8:

- Get everything after hard work, They are very humble and trustworthy, They give more and receive less in life, Hardworking.
- There are blockades in all their endeavors.
- Only after a great struggle, they succeed.
- Tend to give up family life and become renounced.
- Get frustrated, Avoid this name number.

Name number 9:

- Energy, They don't take rest.
- Strong determination for success.
- Their only ideal is to achieve success.
- Always ready to take challenge.
- They are full of worldly experience.
- Do unwanted arguments and fights.
- They study literature. They have willpower and skill in speech.

Name number 10:

- Successful, Dignified and famous.
- They keep on moving.
- They become specialist in something.
- These people are soft-hearted.
- Sometimes, waste time in gossip and unproductive work, Overall good name number.

Name number 11:

- Can get emotional pain.
- They are made for trial and testing.
- Only with a good combination of birth date and name number, they get success. They take up many a job or business.

- They have to be careful in matters involving money.
- They are disappointed with friends and relatives.
- Avoid this name number.

Name number 12:

- May get failure and pain in life.
- They sacrifice for others.
- Get wisdom with growing age.
- They fight for others.
- Have good nature.
- This is rare a number that indicates the possible dangers in advance.
- Sometimes vulnerable.
- Always work for the welfare of others. They share the difficulties of others. Avoid this name number.

Name number 13:

- So many struggles.
- Up down.
- There will be unexpected sorrowful incidents occurring in life, They are learned.
- Have a bad relationship leading to a bad reputation and shame, You think out of the box.
- Sometimes, they have to start from zero after so much success. This number does not have any luck whatsoever.
- Avoid this name number.

Name number 14:

- Success in business.
- People listen to their words and follow them.
- Colorful life, parties and travel is the symbol of your life.
- Good negotiator.

- Having not happy married life.
- They struggle hard while young and achieve great success after that. They earn money from mass communication-oriented business.
- They may waste your energy sometimes. They live a very lucky life.
- Many are waiting to help them.

Name number 15:

- They have every material which is needed.
- Neat clean and glamour.
- They always enjoy help from friends.
- They have a certain power of attraction on their face. Magnetic personality.
- They are achievers.
- They have high energy, so stay young forever.
- They enjoy popularity because of their attractive face. They are very creative, so successful in creative work. They are fashionable and photogenic.

Name number 16:

- They are aggressive, leader and dominating.
- They lodge evil thoughts.
- Their writing has an evil influence.
- They love attention.
- They face disappointment, anger and a fear of fire. Their writing has evil influence.
- They face disappointment, anger and a fear of fire.
- They get quick success.
- They live colorful life.
- In later part of life, problem may arise.

Name number 17:

- They are different.
- This number brings suffering in many different ways. Always ready to take tasks.
- They are tireless workers.
- May face several problems in life.
- Passionate personality.
- Two out of their ten attempts only succeed.
- Failure in some aspect overshadows all the success.
- They are strong people.
- They have a special place of honor in the hearts of people. Controversial life.

Name number 18:

- Some have problems.
- There is an association between the Sun and Saturn in the name number. It indicates negative forces. They face dangers because of indirect enemies, sharp weapons, and bombs.
- Some get easy success.
- They are planned individuals.
- They have lots of inner conflict.
- They are driven to other countries. Good for numbers 1, 3 and 9.

Name number 19:

- This number indicates the successful completion of any endeavour. Good name number.
- Even in advanced age, they look very young.
- As they advance in age, they become persons of great fame and name. They are blessed with success and richness.
- Get wisdom with age.
- They are the bright stars.
- They have so many admirers.

- This is an apex number and indicates continuing greatness.
- They get success easily.
- They are persons of undiminished wealth.
- They love challenges.
- They are leaders.

Name number 20:

- They are very creative, so successful in creative work. Very emotional.
- Those with 20 name number are very calm and peaceful. Constructive and destructive incidents happen in life. They are successful in medication.
- They benefit the whole society with a selfless attitude. Take family responsibility very seriously.
- They may face emotional pain in family matters.
- Avoid this name number.

Name number 21:

- They are lucky, smart and rare personalities.
- This number indicates excessive selfishness.
- They get success and luck.
- They achieve fame, position and wealth.
- They enjoy a permanent job.
- With growing age, they grow in wealth and wisdom.
- They are cunning and planner.
- It is good for a career involving creativity.
- They go beyond the limit to achieve success.

Name number 22:

- It attracts more of the evil than the good.
- They are master of intuition.
- They are successful in litigations. They lose all their wealth because of bad habits. They are lucky and successful.
- They earn and lose money in evil deeds.
- They do not lose heart at the difficulties in life.
- They have a risk if birth number is not compatible with this name number.
- They are multitalented.

Name number 23:

- They are lucky, happy, creative and successful.
- It enables the completion of any assignment.
- They earn the reputation of men of action.
- They succeed in arts. They have a royal status.
- If they are organized and focused, nothing is impossible for them.
- Their greatest challenge is utilization of their talent and gifts in the right proportion. They get help everywhere.
- They are determined and focused.
- Their life is comfortable and peaceful.
- If they take up ordinary tasks, they become lazy and lose the game.
- They have risk of wasting your time.

Name number 24:

- They have every comfort which is needed.
- They are leaders and lucky.
- They become popular in a very short time.
- Magnetic personality and loved by all.
- They have good mental capacity.

- They live a life of duty and dignity.
- They get great fame.
- The status of the life partner will be higher than theirs.
- Control on sensory desires.
- They will gain through a relationship, and the opposite gender brings favor to them. It is one of the luckiest numbers.

Name number 25:

- They love to compete.
- They can foresee anything. They live a disciplined life. They can make an achievement of a challenge.
- They are honest, truthful and devoted to God.
- They are smart and love travelling.
- They earn international fame and reputation.
- Their social life has a glamour effect.
- They are dashing, charismatic and equally dramatic. They are an achiever.
- They try so many businesses and lose their money.

Name number 26:

- They have a problem in a relationship.
- They are spoken ill of for no fault of theirs. Their ambitions are defeated. May have less fertility.
- They take up a venture beyond their capabilities and thus meet with failure. They love travelling.
- Their anger keeps simmering throughout life.
- They are up to anything for the sake of money.
- They may get emotional pain.
- They have a good career.
- They love domestic life and do so much for their family.

Name number 27:

- ▲ This number affords powers of good reputation and rule over land. They have a good fortune in a relationship.
- ▲ They get from masses.
- ▲ It brings about a very affectionate bond between husband and wife. They have good intuition and spiritual knowledge.
- ▲ They have wisdom.
- ▲ They are so emotional.
- ▲ They get involved in holy activities.
- ▲ Don't think much and take action.

Name number 28:

- ▲ They may have emotional pain.
- ▲ It brings ill reputation.
- ▲ They become slaves to evil forces.
- ▲ Wherever they go, they face challenges, jealousy and competition. They advance very fast only to end up in failure.
- ▲ They are career-oriented.
- ▲ They have good intuition.
- ▲ They have good wisdom.
- ▲ It can cause struggle and bad luck.
- ▲ Not a good name number.

Name number 29:

- ▲ They may have emotional pain.
- ▲ Indulge in unnecessary activities and get into trouble, Not good for relationship.
- ▲ They get involved in police complaints.
- ▲ They yield when someone opposes them.

- There is always disagreement between husband and wife. Friends and relatives become ungrateful.
- May caught in argument and legal matter.
- They attract conflict and distrust.

Name number 30:

- They have good mental ability.
- They take up even difficult tasks, just for their satisfaction, even if it has no promise of any profit.
- They have a fertile imagination.
- They are endowed with the powers of thought.
- Good super mind.
- They live a simple life.
- Not interested in making money or earning wealth
- They are soft, emotional and good teachers.
- May have a bad personal life.

Name number 31:

- They have good mental capacity.
- They are business lovers.
- They are very fair and just people.
- They succeed in anything they take up. Name number 31 indicates expertise in arts. They love travel and learning.
- They are not conventional.
- Loves revolution.
- Their life comes across disturbing sad incidents. They are leaders who have clarity.

Name number 32:

- They have a good number.
- This number has the power of irresistible attraction. This number bestows charisma.
- They are known for their intellectual achievements. Have ideas and thoughts.
- Wealthy and down to earth.
- Their eyes have a strong magnetic power. Diplomatic and peacemaker.
- Loves business.
- They may catch in unwanted activities.

Name number 33:

- It is the master number that indicates master teacher.
- They come to have all kinds of wealth.
- They are good in magic, astrology, medicine and spiritual wisdom. Number of wealth and abundance.
- They become happy in helping others.
- They get money in many ways and means.
- They live in a great house. They get very good friends.
- They have a very great spiritual leaning. They are strong people. Their prosperity is always on the increase.
- Their life will be full of comfort and luxuries.
- They are religious and righteous.
- They are very honest.
- This number is a complete package of luck.

Name number 34:

- They are looking for good career.
- Those with 34 as the name number are always interested in having sex. Hardworking and aggressive.
- They are addicts to one thing or the other.
- There are a number of people who talk ill of them behind their backs You have everything for success.
- They are popular and rich.
- But have not a good personal life, which makes their success small.

Name number 35:

- They are popular money minded.
- They are constantly engaged in litigation. Good friends betray them. They are organized.
- Any business in their own name leads to losses.
- They will not get benefits from their family.
- They make money.
- They make their power on those who are under them.
- Not good for personal life.

Name number 36:

- This number leads to great success through hard labour.
- They have good mental capacity.
- Good super mind.
- They have good success in career.
- They are leaders and have good managing ability. Not good for their personal lives.

Name number 37:

- They have good success in their career.
- They are rich and get favor.
- Great powers of popular appeal. It gives a prosperous and comfortable life. Those who stay back in their native place do not enjoy any luck at all.
- They get good position and appreciation.
- They get support from the opposite gender.
- It gives a pleasant life. They become famous in politics and social life. This number brings complete success in a romantic affair.
- They have secret enemy.
- Have good wisdom and intuition.
- Good for occult field.

Name number 38:

- They have struggle.
- As they grow old, their frame, wealth and position keep on moving up. Their emotional approach is not good.
- They may have to suffer because of unexpected dangers.
- Their spiritual powers keep manifest.
- Their spiritual associations keep on increasing.
- Social life is good but overall life is not good. Mixture of luck and bad luck.

Name number 39:

- They can get huge success.
- Name number 39 persons cherish good thoughts.
- Their success lasts for a long.
- They are so good that they will do anything for the good of relatives and friends. They may have to suffer because of skin diseases.
- They have the tenacity to take anything to its successful completion.

- They are a risk taker and get success anyhow.
- Later part of life is good.

Name number 40:

- They are good manager.
- They are people of great intelligence.
- They get a sudden influx of money.
- They utilize resources very well.
- They get success by shortcut otherwise not get it at all. They are good orator and writer.
- Good for initial stage of life.
- Not good in later part of life.

Name number 41:

- They have success.
- This number is a jack of all trades.
- They have capacity to be rich.
- They are good business person.
- They have success in many businesses simultaneously.
- This number has remarkable powers. They are sharp in their intelligence.
- They have great power to govern over people.
- Everyone obeys their words.
- They are successful persons.
- They get great fame.
- They win in competitions very easily.
- They earn international fame. They accomplish historical feats.
- There is a certain attraction about their speech. They live a prosperous life with undiminished fame. They get good positions as a matter of fact. They should not become

egotistic. If they become proud of themselves, they meet with great defeat in life. Number 5 should give up all egotism. They shine well in social life.

- They are very much interested in development.

- They take up many businesses and become great.

Name number 42:

- They have success, comfort, peace and richness.

- They are lucky and supported by everyone.

- Magnetic personality and loved by all.

- They have good mental capacity.

- Control on sensory desires.

- They gain through a relationship, and the opposite gender brings favor to them.

- Right from youth, they have a good physique and are always brisk. They succeed in any endeavor. They have undiminishing wealth. They shine well in politics, arts and social life.

- They are adept at acquiring wealth. They have a great mass appeal. They have the power to subdue others.

Name number 43:

- Gives challenge and struggle.

- They are outspoken, blunt and weird.

- Torture from family and friends.

- They are poor at managing their temperament.

- Not suitable for 4 and 8 numbers.

- All their endeavours finally end in success. Their sorrows are suffered by others. Revolutionary zeal is the weapon for their success. They earn enemies suddenly. They always succeed. There is shrewdness about them. They are also quick in action.

- Their family life is not that very peaceful. They preserve public welfare. They have broad knowledge.

Name number 44:

- They are good in planning and execution. Don't try to involve business in personal lives.
- They are clever, out spoken.
- Sometimes, do wrong deeds to achieve goal.
- Their business may be blocked because of natural calamities. They face danger from water, fire and electricity. They are full of sexual thirst. They shoulder family burdens right at a young age. If they do not control their mind, they go astray through the evil paths and end up in shame and suffering. That brings unmitigated suffering and death-like pain.

Name number 45:

- Good at managing resources.
- People respect them and work under their leadership.
- Good at multitasking.
- They have ability to run a large organization.
- Doing large and grand things. They have the gift of the gab. They take up many a profession. They are tireless workers. They achieve great development and success in their business and profession. They keep a smiling face and speak very engagingly with anyone. They never reveal their personal secret to others. They do not show their difficulties. This number dispels all illnesses.

Name number 46:

- They have good success in their career. They are rich and get favor.
- They become rich and popular. Good for investment.
- They will have good married life.
- Those with 46 as the name number are kings of success. All their plans conceived with nobility of thought definitely succeed. They are idealists. They reach the topmost rung of whatever profession or business they take up. Fame reaches them of its own accord. This number gives high offices in politics. Wherever they go, they will lead others. As they advance in years, their fame, wealth and money keep on the ascent. When they make proper use of their sharp intelligence, they remain the lord of success. They have auspicious powers about them. They get good life partners and good children. They gain an international reputation. Their life is noble and majestic. Those who do not have children

shall make use of this number to become parents. 46 persons shall remain honest in life. That enhances the effect of their luck.

- They get a good life partner and good children. They earn a very good reputation for themselves. They work with a great ideas in their minds. They achieve total success in all that they do. Good positions reach them of their own accord.

Name number 47:

- They are very active and moving and sometimes restless.
- Lives life in different dimensions.
- They think out of the box.
- Side effect on health and emotion.
- Good orator.
- They are likely to suffer from difficulties with sight, headache and even blindness. If they indulge in hunting, they shall give it up. Otherwise, it will entail sin to be carried over to the next birth. Those of name number 47 persons who pursue the path of the divine reach heaven. Their soul is redeemed. They should refrain from sins.

Name number 48:

- They are hard working.
- Religion is very important for them.
- They love social cause.
- Like to help others.
- Sometimes, they have confusion.
- They are particular about matters related to the divine and the spiritual. They have a great liking to take up social service. Fate plays an adverse role in their life. They earn money and wealth but lose it in the course of time. They are very much interested in pilgrimages. Their body and mind are filled with the power of the spiritual.

Name number 49:

- They are leader.
- They plan on everything and most go well.
- This number is not good for personal life.
- Unfortunate events may happen in their life.
- They gain from many businesses.
- They may do illegal things.
- They earn immovable property. They come across many experiences in life and thus become seasoned persons. They get money unexpectedly. They are imaginative. They get money from professions or businesses related to arts. They are subject to accidents. They may even be burnt to death. If the body number and the life number are complementary, they become lucky. Otherwise, they are likely to be attacked by others.

Name number 50:

- They are successful and good planner.
- They work differently from others.
- They have good energy.
- They can foresee things easily.
- They are colorful.
- Learning many things.
- They are the best at teaching others. They are interested in travel. They have the ability to speak effectively. They have special expertise in mathematics, science, astrology and law. They earn huge sums of money with their writings and speeches. They pursue the path of spiritualism diligently. Their life is filled all along with luck.

Name number 51:

- They have struggles.
- As they grow old, their frame, wealth and position keep on moving up. Their emotional approach is not good.
- They may have to suffer because of unexpected dangers.

- Their spiritual powers keep manifest.
- Their spiritual associations keep on increasing.
- Social life is good but overall life is not good. Mixture of luck and bad luck.

Name number 52:

- They can get huge success.
- Name number 39 persons cherish good thoughts.
- Their success lasts for the long.
- They are so good that they will do anything for the good of relatives and friends. They may have to suffer because of skin diseases.
- They have the tenacity to take anything to its successful completion.
- They are risk takers and get success anyhow.
- Later part of life is good.

Name number 53:

- They are good manager.
- They are persons of great intelligence.
- They get a sudden influx of money.
- They utilize resources very well.
- They get success by shortcut otherwise not get it at all. They are good orator and writer.
- Good for the initial stage of life.
- Not good in later part of life.

Name number 54:

- They have success.
- This number is a jack of all trades.
- They have capacity to be rich.
- They are good business people.

- They have success in many businesses simultaneously.
- This number has remarkable powers. They are sharp in their intelligence.
- They have great power to govern over people.
- Everyone obeys their words.
- They are successful persons.
- They get great fame.
- They win in competitions very easily.
- They earn international fame. They accomplish historical feats.
- There is a certain attraction about their speech. They live a prosperous life with undiminished fame. They get good positions as a matter of fact. They should not become egotistic. If they become proud of themselves, they meet with great defeat in life. Number 5 should give up all egotism. They shine well in social life.
- They are very much interested in development.
- They take up many businesses and become great.

Name number 55:

- They have success, comfort, peace and richness.
- They are lucky and supported by everyone.
- Magnetic personality and loved by all.
- They have good mental capacity.
- Control on sensory desires.
- They gain through a relationship and the opposite gender brings favor to them.
- Right from youth, they have a good physique and are always brisk. They succeed in any endeavor. They have undiminishing wealth. They shine well in politics, arts and social life.
- They are charismatic personalities. There is life in their speech. Great positions seek them. They live a famous life. They have the power to subdue others. They are full of desires. They are thrifty. They amass all forms of wealth. They are full of courage, willpower and self-confidence. They have an ever-increasing spiritual power. When they resist the temptation to be selfish, their health is ensured. They have a strong body. Many responsible

positions come in search of them. Whatever illness they may feel is almost immediately cured. They have a majestic look. This number is the luckiest one. They get money, position and fame. They live with a lot of fame.

- They are adept at acquiring wealth. They have a great mass appeal. They have the power to subdue others.

Name number 56:

- Gives challenge and struggle.

- They are outspoken, blunt and weird.

- Torture from family and friends.

- They are poor at managing their temperament.

- Not suitable for 4 and 8 numbers.

- All their endeavours finally end in success. Their sorrows are suffered by others. Revolutionary zeal is the weapon for their success. They earn enemies suddenly. They always succeed. There is shrewdness about them. They are also quick in action.

- Their family life is not that very peaceful. They preserve public welfare. They have broad knowledge.

Name number 57:

- They are good at planning and execution. Don't try to involve business in their personal life.

- They are clever, outspoken.

- Sometimes, do wrong deeds to achieve goals.

- Their business may be blocked because of natural calamities. They face danger from water, fire and electricity. They are full of sexual thirst. They shoulder family burdens right at a young age. If they do not control their mind, they go astray through the evil paths and end up in shame and suffering. That brings unmitigated suffering and death-like pain.

Name number 58:

- Good at managing resources.

- People respect them and work under their leadership.

- Good at multitasking.

- They have ability to run a large organization.

- Doing large and grand things. They have the gift of the gab. They take up many a profession. They are tireless workers. They achieve great development and success in their business and profession. They keep a smiling face and speak very engagingly with anyone. They never reveal their personal secret to others. They do not show their difficulties. This number dispels all illnesses.

Name number 59:

- They have good success in careers. They are rich and get favor.

- They become rich and popular. Good for investment.

- They will have a good married life.

- Those with 46 as the name number are kings of success. All their plans conceived with the nobility of thought definitely succeed. They are idealists. They reach the topmost rung of whatever profession or business they take up. Fame reaches them of its own accord. This number gives high offices in politics. Wherever they go, they will lead others. As they advance in years, their fame, wealth and money keep on the ascent. When they make proper use of their sharp intelligence, they remain the lord of success. They have auspicious powers about them. They get good life partners and good children. They gain an international reputation. Their life is noble and majestic. Those who do not have children shall make use of this number to become parents. 46 persons shall remain honest in life. That enhances the effect of their luck.

- They get a good life partners and good children. They earn a very good reputation for themselves. They work with a great idea in their minds. They achieve total success in all that they do. Good positions reach them of their own accord.

Name number 60:

- They are very active and moving and sometimes restless.
- Lives life in different dimensions.
- They think out of the box.
- Side effect on health and emotion.
- Good orator.
- They are likely to suffer from difficulties with sight, headache and even blindness. If they indulge in hunting, they shall give it up. Otherwise, it will entail sin to be carried over to the next birth. Those of name number 47 persons who pursue the path of the divine reach heaven. Their soul is redeemed. They should refrain from sins.

Name number 61:

- They are hard working.
- Religion is very important for Them.
- They love social causes.
- Likes to help others.
- Sometimes They have confusion.
- They are particular about matters related to the divine and the spiritual. They have a great liking to take up social service. Fate plays an adverse role in their life. They earn money and wealth but lose it in the course of time. They are very much interested in pilgrimages. Their body and mind are filled with the power of the spiritual.

Name number 62:

- They are leader.
- They plan on everything and most go well.
- This number is not good for personal life.
- Unfortunate events may happen in their life.
- They gain from many businesses.
- They may do illegal things.

- ⋏ They earn immovable property. They come across many experiences in life and thus become seasoned persons. They get money unexpectedly. They are imaginative. They get money from professions or businesses related to arts. They are subject to accidents. They may even be burnt to death. If the body number and the life number are complementary, they become lucky. Otherwise, they are likely to be attacked by others.

Name number 63:

- ⋏ They are a successful and good planner.
- ⋏ They work differently from others.
- ⋏ They have good energy.
- ⋏ They can foresee things easily.
- ⋏ They are colorful.
- ⋏ Learning many things.
- ⋏ They are the best at teaching others. They are interested in travel. They have the ability to speak effectively. They have special expertise in mathematics, science, astrology and law. They earn huge sums of money with their writings and speeches. They pursue the path of spiritualism diligently. Their life is filled all along with luck.

Kua Number (Angel Number)

Kua Number is a basic concept in Loshu. Kua number is calculated based on the Date of Birth and Gender of a person. According to LOSHU, the year of birth of a person has some influence on certain qualities, abilities and features of the individual. It is also believed that a better understanding of Kua Number helps in the development of a person's potential and also the overall improvement of his life.

How to calculate Kua Number?

Calculation of Kua Number is based on a simple formula. For the calculation of Feng shui kua, 2 factors are taken into consideration - Year of birth and Gender. Follow these simple steps to calculate Kua Number:

- Add the last two digits of your year of birth. If the resulting number is a double digit, add the digits once again to get a single digit.

- **Kua Number for female** – Add 5 to the single digit obtained in the previous step. If the result is a double-digit, add the digits to get a single digit number.

- **Kua Number for male** - Subtract the single digit obtained in the first step from 10. The resulting single-digit number will give the Feng shui kua number for male.

- For Example, if your year of birth is 1982 add the last two digits, ie., 8+2=10, which is a double-digit number. Therefore add the two digits, 1 + 0 = 1.

- For calculating the Kua number of a Male, subtract 1 from 10. Therefore Kua number for male born in 1982 is 10 - 1 = 9.

- For females, add 5 to the number obtained in first step. 1+5=6. Therefore, Feng Shui Kua Number of a female born in 1982 is 6.

Kua Number 1

Positive Traits

Great willpower

Flexible

Self-sufficient

Creative

Helpful to those around them

Negative Traits

Overly emotional Needy Temperamental

Critical Self-indulgent

Best Colors

Black

Blue

Kua Number 3

Positive Traits

Patient

Works well under pressure

Makes good leader

Intelligent

Organized

Open-minded

Ability to grow beyond current limitations

Negative Traits

Self-absorbed

Stubborn

Inability to adapt Manipulative

Ingrown and closed-minded

Best Colors

Green

Blue

Black

Brown

Kua Number 4

Positive Traits

Pragmatic

Organized

Loyal

Love learning new things Open-minded

Negative Traits

Demanding Arrogant Judgmental Disloyal Opinionated

Best Colors

Green

Blue

Black

Brown

Kua Number 9

Positive Traits

Charismatic Passionate Energetic Enthusiastic Persuasive

Negative Traits

Combative Argumentative Overindulgent Easily excitable Lackluster

Best Colors

Red

Purple

Pink

Green

Kua Number 2

Positive Traits

Honest

Stable Reliable Hard-working Confident

Negative Traits

Blunt

Set in ways

Workaholic

Takes on too much responsibility Insecure

Best Colors

Beige

Yellow

Orange

Russet

Kua Number 5

The Kua number 5 is divided into male and female since it represents the combination of yin and yang chi energies. To accomplish this, each gender is reassigned a different Kua number:

Males will use the Kua number 2. Females will use the Kua number 8. Kua Number 6

Positive Traits

Insightful Knowledgeable Analytical Focused Goal-oriented

Negative Traits

Withdrawn

Defensive

Easily depressed Emotionally unavailable

Ambitionless

Best Colors

Yellow

White

Gold

Gray

Silver

Kua Number 7

Positive Traits

Optimistic Artistic Graceful Level-headed Visionary

Negative Traits

Picky Self-absorbed Defensive Emotionally repressed Unreasonable

Best Colors

Yellow

Beige

Brown

Gold

Silver

Copper

Kua Number 8

Positive Traits

Focused Goal-oriented

Great problem solvers

Visionary Creative

Negative Traits

Manipulative

Greedy

Stubborn

Resistant to change Unable to advance in life

Best Colors

Yellow

Beige

Brown

Red

Pink

Purple

Personality and Kua Numbers

There is much more that goes into forming your personality than just your Kua number. Your unique life experiences, philosophical beliefs, and environment also play a role in who you are. Your personal Kua number can provide insight into the foundation of your personality traits to enhance your life and relationships.

Vedic Numerology

Vedic Numerology is also called Ank Jyotish, just like Loshu Grid it has a bit different number combination in grid. It is also associated with number in Laxmi Ganesh Yantra; Maa Laxmi signifies wealth and Ganesh signifies power wisdom knowledge. Maa Laxmi is one of prayed goddessess in Indian culture, without Maa Laxmi, existence of human beings is not possible, so as Vedic grid is helpful for calculating the most detailed life events. This Loshu Grid has more accuracy as compared to Loshu Grid, so it is more popular among Numerologist. Vedic numerology is based on belief that positions of celestial bodies at the time of birth can influence their behavious and destiny. It involved the study of positions of planets and stars.

3	1	9
6	7	5
2	8	4

In Vedic Numerology, sum total of date of birth is called Life Path number or Destiny number; it reflects a person's Career, Talent, Challenges in life and so on. This number also helps to find a true purpose and career. In vedic numerology, Concept of MADASHA, ANTARDASHA & PRATYANTAR dasha play major roles for calculation; Madahsa is the longest time period when a single planet resides in a persons life the day he or she born, for example, dob 27/8/1993 the First maha dasha that comes according to the dob is 27=2+7=9, so for 9 years, Mars maha dasha will be there from 27/8/1993 to 27/8/2002, and after 27/8/2002 Sun maha will be there, as after 9 cycles repeat from 1 to 9. So next Mahadasha would be 27/8/2002 to 27/8/2003 Sun mahadasha.

Thereafter Madasha, there is another Dasha called Antar dasha. Antar dasha is Shorter time period; the dasha or plant revolves in the person's life for every birthday; the Antardasha changes and finally comes Pratyantar dasha. When it is Dasha under dasha, it is dasha that comes on monthly or in basic of days in very short duration, but it's impacts are same as Mahdasha, so should not be ignored .

Madasha → (Sub period) → Antardasha → (SUB-SUB Period) Pratyantar Daha

Madasha detail calculation

Example - JUNE 8th 1993

Basic no : 8, Destiney 6+8+1+9+9+3=36=9

MADASHA

June 8 1993 - June 7 2001:8 (Saturn)

June 8 2001 - June 7 2010:9 (Mars)

June 8 2010 - June 7 2011:1 (Sun)

June 8 2011 - June 7 2013:2 (Moon)

June 8 2013 - June 7 2016:8 (Jupiter)

June 8 2013 - June 7 2020:4 (Rahu)

June 8 2020 - June 7 2025:5 (Mecury)

June 8 2025 - June 7 2031:6 (Venus)

June 8 2031 - June 7 2038:7 (Ketu)

It is calculated further from Saturn 8 and so on…

For Antar Dasha Calculation, we have to follow a table

Number	Planet	Day of the week
1	Sun	Sunday
2	Moon	Monday
3	Jupiter	Thursday
4	Rahu	-
5	Mercury	Wednesday
6	Venus	Friday
7	Ketu	-
8	Saturn	Saturday
9	Mars	Tuesday

Antardasha

June 8 2022

For Antar dasha, let's imagine for current year 2022. First carefully find what day on 8/06/2022, it is on (Wednesday) 8/6/2022 we have to remove Century, which is 20 in our case. For every birthday, Antardasha changes.

8/6/2022, Do not consider 20 and add

8+6+2+2+ (Day of the week)

8+6+2+2+(5) = 23

2+3 = 5

From June 8, 2022, Antardasha is Mercury, which is 5.

Pratyantar Dasha

For example, 8/6/2022. As this person's Antardahsa is 5 (Mercury), the closing of Antar dasha, that is 5 (Mercury), is beginning of Pratyantar daha, which is also 5 Mercury.

8/6/2022: AD = 5 (Mercury)

We have to Multiply 5(AD)*5=25 (8/06/2023) + 25 Days = July 3rd 2022

Pratyantar Dasha

08/06/2022 - 03/7/2022:Mercury (5*5=25 days)   add 25 days to

04/07/2022 - 02/08/2022:Venus (5*6=30 days)   add 30 days

03/08/2022 - 06/09/2022:Ketu (5*7=35 days)   add 35 days

07/09/2022 - 16/10/2022:Saturn (5*8=40 days)   add 40 days

17/10/2022 - 30/11/2022:Mars (5*9=45 days)   add 45 days

01/12/2022 - 5/12/2022: Sun (5*1=5 days)   add 5 days

06/12/2022 - 15/12/2022:Moon (5*2=10 days)   add 10 days

16/12/2022 - 30/12/2022:Jupiter (5*3=15 days)   add 15 days

31/12/2022 - 19/01/2023:Rahu (5*4=20 days)   add 20 days

28/01/2023 - 23/02/2023: Mercury (5*5=25 days) add 25 days

14/02/2023 - 15/03/2023:Venus (5*6=30 days)   add 30 days

16/03/2023 - 19/4/2023: Ketu (5*7=35 days)   add 35 days

20/04/2023 - 30/5/2023: Saturn (5*8=40 days)   add 40 days

After Saturn, there is Mars Dasha; it is a passed person's DOB that is 5*9= 45, so we ignore rest of the days.

31/05/2023 - june 7, 2023 = Mars

June 8, 2023 New Antardasha

New Prtyantardasha

June 8th 2022

MD:5

AD:5

PD:5 Till July 3rd

For Example: Putting numbers on the grid for DOB June 8, 2022.

MD:5

AD:5

PD:5 till July 3rd

Original DOB 8/06/1993 with Birth number 8 and Destiny number 9.

So we ignore Century number as per Vedic Numerology rule.

3	1	99
6		5MD, 5AD, 5PD
	8, 8	

Vedic Grid various planes

3-1-9 - Name & Fame, Intellectual, Socialpresence, Professional & Career.

6-7-5 – They are into good business, Mind Plane, Luxury, Bollywood Celebrity.

2-8-4 - Success from hard work, Ground level, Lots of struggle.

3-6-2 - Planner, Education, Memory sharp, Good communication, Public speaker, leaders.

1-7-8 - Spiritual, Social Circle, Creative, They have very good money, They help easily to others but they didn't get help back.

9-5-4 - Actionplane, Actfast, Decision making capacity, IT Sector, Good communication, Capacity of Brain wash.

3-7-4 – Success.

9-7-2-Courage, Fearless.

Vedic Grid & importance of Numbers

Cash Flow, Freedom Lover Action

3		9
6		5

Arts & Creativity, Beautiful

6		
2		

Communication, Litigation

		5
		4

Nobel Heart, Good luck yog, Raj yog, Govt. job possibility

	1	
	7	

Spirituality, Struggle and Hard work

	7	
	8	

Confusion, Hard work, Suicidal thoughts

2	8	

Determination, Accident yog, Major loss of Life, Family Disturbance

	8	4

Argumentative, Easy money yog, Good in Occult science

	7	5

Lack of Interest, Possibility of Affairs, Poor health Management

6	7	

(Vedic Grid & importance Drishti)

Philosophical nature, highly intelligent and wisdom seeker, Judgmental analytical skills are good, multi-talented

3		
2		

Jupiter & Moon number number between them

		9
		4

Mangal and Rahu number between them

Strong willpower, Extreme Dominating, Strong goal conversion capability can go to any extreme for success, Hospitalization, Litigation Ups and Downs in career, Ego-less personality, Financial instability, Sun & Saturn in opposite, no Number between them.

	1	
	8	

Good Counsellor, Consultant, Spiritual development, Interest in occult science, Success after hard work.

3		
	8	

Jupiter & Saturn are Retro aspect

	1	
		4

Family issues, Up and down in career Wasteful expenditure

		9
	8	

Good Humanitarian, Avg. self-confidence, Unable to make decisions, Hard work credit are taken by others.

Mars and Saturn, When Mars and Saturn are retroaspect.

	1	
2		

Mood swing, Sensitive in nature, Family Issues, Ups and Downs in career

When the Sun and Moon are in retro aspect.

Vedic Grid-Quadrangular Relationship

	1	
6		5
	8	

Intelligent, good Willpower, Courage, Name and Fame in Society, Good Financial success, Problems in relationships, Unhappy Married Life.

When 1, 5, 8 & 6 Quadrangle is formed.

Vedic Grid-L Shape-175

	1	
	7	5

Emotional, Logical Mind, Argumentative, Problems in relationships with others.

When 1, 7 & 5 L Shape is formed by Sun-Ketu-Mercury.

Vedic Grid-L Shape 1-3-6

3	1	
6		

Highly intellectual knowledge, Wisdom, Good in teaching, Luck after marriage, Good growth and expansion in career.

When 1, 3 & 6 L-Shape is formed by sun-venus-Jupiter.

Vedic Grid-L Shape 1-9-7

	1	9
	7	

Success and Honour in career, Aggressive nature, Strong willpower, Good Risktaker, Abroad settlement.

When 1, 9 & 7 L-Shape is formed by Sun-Mars-Ketu.

Vedic Grid-L Shape 7-5-4

	7	5
		4

Struggle in life, Hard worker, Achieve success after hard work, Weak communication skills.

When 7, 5 & 4 L-Shape is formed by Ketu-Mer-RAHU.

Vedic Grid-L Shape 1-9-5

	1	9
		5

Straight forward personality, Very Intelligent, Aggressive and dominating, Enthusiastic, Good motivator, Communication skill is good.

When 1, 9 & 5 L-Shape is formed by Sun, Mar, Mercury.

Vedic Grid-L Shape 5-8-4

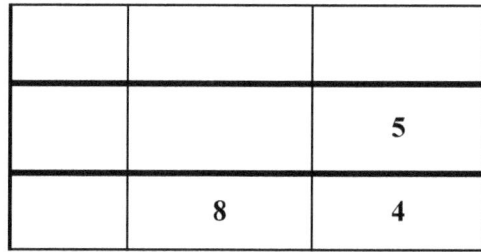

Kind-hearted and Good humanitarian, Confused mind, UP and Down in career, Poor relationships with others.

When 5, 8 & 4 L-Shape is formed by Mer-Satu-Rahu.

Vedic Grid-L Shape 6-2-8

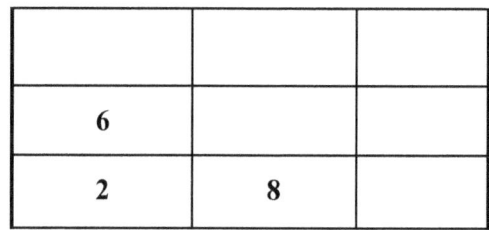

Good Economic Status and success, Unhappy married life, Chances of late marriage, Very Emotional and Sensitive person.

When 6, 2 & 8 L-Shape is formed by Venus-Moon-Saturn.

Suitable Profession

Number	Profession
1	Govt Jobs, IAS, Politics, Entrepreneur, Industrialist, Doctor, School Owner, Agriculture, Scientist, Innovator, Computer Programmer, Administration, Advisor.
2	Purchase Manager, Vendor development, Supply chain management, Diplomat, Language Translator, Librarian, Placement Agency, Travel Industry, Diary Business, Pharmacist, Nursing, Research/Data Analyst, Engineer, HR Manager, Homemaker, Host/Hostess.
3	Project Planning & Management, Advertising (creatives), Copyrighting, Editing, Business Strategists, Teaching & Education, Content Development, Electronics, Agriculture.
4	Real Estate Developer, Industrialist, Glamour Industry, Jeweler, Lawyer, Doctor, Religious Rituals (Karam Kand), Pathology, XRay Lab.
5	Trading, Astrologer, IT, Sales, Marketing, Public Speaking, Teacher, Accountancy, PrintingIndustry, Editing, Investigation, Commission, Liaison work, Marriage Bureau.
6	Acting, Interior decorator, Fashion designer, Beauty & Luxury, Products (Artificial Jewelry, Cosmetics, Ladies Products etc), Management, any work which involve beautification.
7	Occult Sciences (Vastu Consultant, Numerologists, Tarotetc), Research Scientists, Interior Designer, Counsellor.
8	Chartered Accountant, Finance, Banking, Steel Industry, Media, PR, Sports, Footwear, Politics, Real Estate Dealer, Fund Manager.
9	Physiotherapy, Police, Army, Lower Management, Factory Production/Technical, Real Estate Developer, Post which has power, like Police, Army, Judge etc.

Personal Year, Month & Date

Personal Year - In Numerology, the personal year number is used to give you a brief synopsis of what you can expect in the upcoming year. According to Numerology, every thing in the Universe is made up of vibrational energy.

Personal Year Calculation-

Birth Day+Birth Month+Current Year

Example1-03-12-1982 (2024) Current year 1+ 3+1+2+8=14=5 **Personal Year**

Personal Year Calculation

Birth Day+Birth Month+Current Year Example 223-06-1986 (Current year 2023)

2+3+0+6+2+0+2+3=18=1+9= 10 = 1 **Personal Year**

Personal Year - Number wise Meanings

Personal Year 1 - New Beginnings, New Foundation, Promotion, Honor, Full Speed may not be good for **Driver 8,** New energy year. This year decission-making power is more, Pending work completion year, Never hesitate to connect to new people, Ask for help in case of ego and avoid over-confidence.

Personal Year 2 - Relationship & Partnership, Patience, Slow & gentle year, consolidation year, Mental tension not good for – **4, 8, 9 & 6.** Don't make emotional decisions, Avoid new projects, Increase in knowledge and research this year, Don't disclose plans this year.

Personal Year 3 - Social activities, Creativity, friendship, Good for Study, Late delivery, Good for Spiritual, Will give result after 3-4 Months, Not Good for **Driver 6,** Travel opportunities, New friends meeting, Love affairs this year, Get recognition this year.

Personal Year 4 - Year of Hard work, Personal discipline, Sudden loss & gain, it's subject to goal setting if you are subject to goal setting; if you are done, Not good for **2, 8 & 9,** Investment in real estate or home renovation this year is good.

Personal Year 5 - Year of Change, Travel, Fun & Expansion, Expect the unexpected, Impossible might be possible this year, Marriage, Divorce, New house will be there, Alcohol, Drugs, Physical intimacy will be more this year, so it should be taken care.

Personal Year 6 - Year of Home, Family & Marriage, Neither good nor bad, Year of gain, Best for unmarried people, Year of home decoration, Not good for driver **3**, Year of love affair, New house, New job, Health issues will be more this year.

Personal Year 7 - Year of search for great meaning & purpose of your life, Spirituality, Personal development, No Material gain–**Good For Everyone**, Up and down this year or turbulence if no spirituality practices, Never expand business this year, Not good for new decisions, Meeting old friends this year, Need to face old problems this year, Religious tour this year, Loneliness in this year, but not get into depression.

Personal Year 8 - Year of Money, Power, & Business, Switch from old business to new, May give health problem, Not good for driver **1, 8 & 9,** Year of hard work, To sale property, it is a good year, Property investment might be possible, Year of Money recovery.

Personal Year 9 - Year of completion & ending, Consolidation, Audit year or punishment year, Year of looking/or not to take action not good for 4, 6, 8, 2, Don't involve in litigation, Don't take hasty decissions, Personal year 9 might get surgeries.

Personal Year of famous celebrities, Sports persons & Politicians.

Name	Personal Year for 2024 Birth Day+Birth Month+Current Year
Amitabh Bacchan (Actor) 11/10/1942	2
Narendra Modi (Politician) 17/9/1950	7
Virat Kohli (Sports Person) 5/11/1988	6
Rohit Sharma (Sports person) 30/4/1987	6

Salman Khan (Actor) 27/12/1965	2
David Bekhum (Sports Person) 2/5/1975	6
Amit Shah (Politician) 22/10/1964	5
Hema Malini (Actor, Politician) 16/10/1948	7
Mukesh Ambani 19/4/1957	4
Ratan Tata-28/12/1937	4

Personal Month

January	1
February	2
March	3
April	4
May	5
June	6
July	7
August	8
September	9
October	10

Personal Month Calculation-

Personal Year Number+Current Year Month

In case of 03/12/1982

Personal year is 5, Current month is from 1/1/2024

Month	For year 2024
January	5+1=6
November	11=2
December	12=3

In Numerology, the Personal Year Number is used to give you a brief synopsis of what you can expect for the upcoming year. According to Numerology, everything in the Universe is made up of vibrational energy. Personal number to each month.

February	5+2=7
March	5+3=8
April	5+4=9
May	5+5=10=1
June	5+6=11=2
July	5+7=12=3
August	5+8=13=4
September	5+9=14=5
October	5+10=15=6
November	5+11=16=7
December	5+12=17=8

Personal Day

Personal Day Calculation-

Personal Month+Current month date

Example 1- if Dob 3-12-1982

Personal Year – 3+1+2+2+0+2+4= 14=5

If Current Month is date 1 Dec 2024

Personal Month = 5+3=8

Personal day is 8+1 = 9 Personal date

Personal date and month is very important in case of calculating day-to-day activities and comparing these dates to your Driver number and Conductor number, for more deep analysis as per numerology in Vedic Grid also used to find auspicious days and months.

Number	Profession
1	Avoid all work of 8
2	Avoid all work of 4 and 8
3	Avoid all work of 6
4	Avoid all work of 2 and 9
5	Can do all work
6	Avoid all work of 3
7	No partnership rest do whatever u like
8	Avoid all work of 2 and 1
9	Avoid all work of 4 and 8

Missing number & their remedies, Number 1 & Health Issues

Numbers, that are completely missing from the chart, indicate a lesson that the person has to learn in his lifetime. Knowing what numbers, friends and families are missing in their chart allows us to know what they are struggling to learn. This enables us to be more understanding and supportive. With this knowledge, we might file others for their performance in certain areas. By knowing their missing numbers, we can encourage and help them in their difficult areas and encourage them to lead a more successful life. Everyone has at least one number missing in his or her chart.

Number 1 denotes to **planet Sun**, which is the head of the solar planet and an important **source of energy.**

- Apart from the main Planet number & Life Path number, if number 1 is present in Lo Shu Grid that makes a person helpful and energetic.

Remedies–

- Name on number 1 will be helpful.
- Offering water to the Sun and chanting Surya Mantra.
- Try to repeat number 1 in your life again and again, like in the house number, mobile number, vehicle number, etc.
- Keep Fountain/Aquarium in the North corner of the house.
- Tie Red thread on your wrist in the right hand.

Health ISSUE–

- Heart disease, Urine disorder, Head, Neck, Eye issues and Teeth Related issues.

Solution – Low salt, more physical work, avoid late-night dinner.

Missing number & their remedies, Health issue – Number 2

Number 2 denotes to planet Moon, considered as queen in numerology, which reflects the light of the Sun. Moon controls emotion and like a queen, the moon also denotes a mother, which shows intuitive power and mood swings, too. People with number 2 are good at doing donations and helping others.

Remedies–

- They can wear Pearl or can wear Mala of Crystals.
- Chanting Shiv mantra will be good.
- Drinking water in a silver glass will be good.
- Hang pictures of mountains without water in the South-West corner of the house.
- Give daan (donate) of Rice or Sugar.

Health ISSUE–

- Lung Related issues, Tumer, Mental disorder, Gastric problem.

Solution – Green vegetable, Banana & Fruits, Water on the head side and dispose it off in the morning, Kali Mirch & Honey, Avoid Coffee & Tobaco, Use lemon.

Missing number & their remedies, Health issue – Number 3

Number 3 denotes to planet Jupiter, which is considered as an ancestor, minister, teacher and advisor in the numerology chart.

Jupiter is the biggest planet and contains a lot of information within. Jupiter increases curiosity to learn new things and share experiences and knowledge with others. Also, Jupiter increases interest in Spirituality and occult.

Remedies–

- Wearing turmeric mala will be good.
- Worshiping the banana tree on Thursday will be helpful.
- Applying saffron tilak will be helpful.
- As number 3 represents the Wood element, the person should put Sceneries of the green plant in the East of the House.
- They can wear Tulsi mala of five Mukhi Rudraksha.
- They should always respect old people and teachers.

Health ISSUE–

- Throat disease, Skin Disease, Paralysis, Nervous system, Back pain and Leg pain, Cough issues.

Solution – Apple, Cheery, Grapes, Saffron.

Missing number & their remedies with Health impact–Number 4

Number 4 is planet Rahu, which is considered as the upper body part.

Rahu gives powerful mind and logical thinking. It gives the power to think logically. People with number 4 are generally good at calculation and always plan.

All body power remains in the mind only. Sometimes, they can't stop thinking, which can create a disturbance in sleeping.

Remedies–

- Using wooden elements/keeping a wooden pen or pencil along with you will be good. Do Nariyal daan.
- Give food to strays.
- Always keep your feet clean.
- Keep green plant sceneries in South-East.
- Help dogs, serve them.

Health ISSUE – Knee problems, Below Stomach, Neck pain, Leg-Related issues, Arthritis, Infection very fast.

Solution – Green Vegetable, Fruits use after sunset, Take 2-3 Opinion, Take safety majors.

Missing number & their remedies with Health issues–Number 5

Number 5 denotes planet Mercury. In numerology, Mercury is considered as a Prince, which has the blessings of elders. These people are loved and They make friends easily. Also, Mercury is the planet for communication and balance in life. In Loshu Grid, it takes the central place, which means no enmity.

Mercury gives the courage to speak in public.

Remedies–

- Keep name on number 5.
- Wear green clothes on Wednesday.
- Sit in the sunlight daily for 10 minutes.
- There should be no electric item in the center of the house.

Health ISSUE – Nervous System issue, Indigestion, Weak eye-sight, Arm and Shoulder pain, Paralysis problems, Neck to Waist between issues, Insomnia issue.

Solution – Carrot, Worship to Lord Ganesh.

Missing number & their remedies Number 6

Number 6 denotes the planet Venus, which is considered as Guru for the evil planets. Venus shows the right path.

Venus gives for entertainment and luxury in life. People with Venus planet are good counsellors too. Venus helps in getting love and care from your life partner.

Remedies–

- Name on number 6.
- Donate something to a lady on Friday.
- Chanting of Shukra Mantra and worshipping of Shukra Yantra.
- They should wear a watch or bracelet with a Golden chain. They can also try to wear Yellow clothes while going for some important work.
- They should respect ladies. Give cosmetics gift to the married woman.

- Keep 11 long 6 rods of golden wind chime hanging in North-West.

Health ISSUE – Heart-related Problems, Heartbreak, Nose, Upper lungs, cold all the time, Kidney issues.

Solution – Use Skhura yantra.

Missing number & their remedies– Number 7

Number 7 denotes planet Ketu, which refers only lower body, Ketu does not have eyes, so always follow the heart.

People with number 7 are generally emotional, Have good 6th sense. Also, number 7 keeps the people grounded and cool in every tough situation.

Remedies–

- Wearing a gold & silver mixed chain wristwatch will be good.
- Chanting of Shree Ganesh Mantra.
- Hanga wind chime in the west of 11 Inch 5 Or 6 rods of a mix of silver & golden color.
- Help dogs, serve them.
- They should wear light color clothes such as white, light blue, light green.

Health ISSUE – Anxiety, Insomnia, Eye-related issues, Overthinking, Stomach Problems, Skin issues.

Solution – Avoid late-night working & Give Time to Family, Play to get rid of Health issues.

Missing number & their remedies–Number 8

Number 8 denotes planet Saturn. Saturn is the slowest moving planet, people with the number 8 are generally considered as **slow growth.** People with the number 8 in their chart will always get the result of their actions. Also, number 8 is about the **law and regulation.**

Remedies–

- Light up a mustard oil diya under a peepal tree after sunset.
- Donate black pulse.
- Massage feet soul with mustard oil.
- Educate others with their knowledge.

- They should respect labour or lower-class people.
- Distribute salty food.
- They should not eat nonveg on Saturdays, rather do fasting on Saturdays.

Health ISSUE – Surgeries, Ear, Leg issues, Bones issues, Paralysis issue.

Missing number & their remedies–Number 9

Number 9 denotes to planet Mars, which is considered a Commander number. People with number 9, have good self-belief and take responsibility from an early age.

People with the number 9 generally have a fighter attitude and are aggressive. They have the energy to work and also motivate others for growth.

Remedies–

- Read Hanuman chalisa daily.
- Apply orange sindoor tilak on the forehead.
- Give bananas to monkeys.
- Drink water in copper.
- Put fire pictures, keep red blub in the South.
- Visit the Hanuman temple.

Health ISSUE–

Accident Prone, Injuries, Fracture, Surgeries, Bleeding, Kidney, Throat infection.

Solution – Prefer Sports for Energy channelized, Donate blood, Avoid alcohol.

Various Important Combination:

> 3, 4 Missing

No Financial growth

> 6, 7 Missing

Have to do everything without any support. Do not get pleasure in life.

> 2, 5, 8 missing

Can't make a house with foundation.

Should make house after 48 years with foundation.

- ➢ 1 Missing

Can't do planning properly, less water in the body.

- ➢ 6, 7, 3, 4 Missing

Too much struggle.

- ➢ 9 missing

No excitement, No technical mind, No name and fame and No recognition.

Missing complete line in grid.

Too much struggle and indicating dosh in Kundali.

- ➢ Missing 5

Sensitive stomach, back pain, no confidence.

- ➢ Any one number missing from 2, 5, 8

Can't make a house with foundation, so they mostly live in such house which is not connected to land.

- ➢ 7 present number presents Support from Family.

Mobile Numerology

In the era of globalization, mobile phone is one of an essential part of our lives and smart phones not only make a piece of cake in terms of connectivity but their numbers also have miracle result in Health, Weath and relationship. Each Mobile number is energy to connect to outer world, so these numbers should synchronize with each other for better work ability either in relation, Business, or career. Mobile numerology is a combination of numbers and their study, as per numerology 11 numbers; their number combination and ending also lead to results either good or bad or neutral.

Just as in numerology, each number from 1 to 9 has characteristics mobile numbers also have the same:

Mobile no	Characteristics	Suitable profession
1	Power	CEOs, Enterprenuers
2	Caring, Romantic	Artists
3	Management	Teachers, Writers, Spiritual leaders
4	Instability	Scientists, Media professsionals
5	Transformation, Communication	Businessmen
6	Family number	Home makers, Actors
7	Research-oriented, Thinkers	Researchers
8	Good for people working for masses	Lawyers, Educators, Finance professionals
9	Fortunate but avoid in case of health issues	Health care workers, Leaders

Always fill your missing numbers in Mobiles numbers for blessing

- Don't take anti-numbers in Mobile numbers.
- Try to not take 2, 4 & 8 in your mobile numbers, especially in the last 3 Digits.
- Recommended number in last 11/111/111, 55/555, 33/333 or 55/555/5555.
- If you have 3 Driver or Conductor, don't take sum of 6 and the last digit 66/666.
- If you have 6 Driver or Conduct or never take 3 in total and 33 or 333.
- If You have Driver or conductor 8 don't take last digit 11/111/1111 or total 1.
- 5 Numbers can go anywhere or everywhere.
- For Business, take 1, 3, 5 & 7 in the last and total sum to numbers.

Mobile no combination analysis

For Example, mobile no 7987153950

Make a pair of each number

79, 98, 87, 71, 15, 53, 39, 95, 50

How to select the perfect mobile number as per numerology?

Calculating the mobile number, as per numerology, involves by assigning numerical value to each number and adding them to single number; as per numerology, country code is not considered in case of calculation; the following steps to be considered before selecting a mobile number.

Step 1 - Write the mobile number excluding country code, for example, +91 7987153950, Here, the country code is 91 to remove and write number 7987153950. For example, consider driver and conductor numbers 5 & 9.

Step 2 – Assign a numerical value to each digit according to numerology.

0=0

1=1

2=2

3=3

4=4

5=5

6=6

7=7

8=8

9=9

Step 3 - Add all digits of the mobile number and sum total to single digit number, for example,

7+9+8+7+1+5+3+9+5+0=54 = 9

Therefore, Mobile number, given mobile number is 9

Step 4 - Pairing of numbers in 2s

79, 98, 87, 71, 15, 53, 39, 95, 50

Interpret each number with a positive and negative results; if more than 3 negative numbers, it should be avoided; if in case the above mobile number is of health care professional and total is 9 and the conductor number is 27 and total is 9, so could consider this number as positive.

- **12/21** - Good growth, good instability, mood swings, unnecessary expenses.
- 14-41 - loss of money, Defamation.
- 15-51 - Helpful in married life support, earn money with less effort.
- 16/61 - Money loss job loss, small accidents, partner health issue.
- 17/71 - Help in Government jobs, Working for corporates.
- 18/81 - Career and Money Ups and Downs, Disputes with father and son.
- 19/91 - Good leadership quality, Higher education.
- 23/32 - Extra Marital connection.
- 24/42 - Mood swings negative mindset, Unnecessary busy in work.
- 28/82 - Possibility of depression, Issues with partnership.
- 34/43 - Strong willpower, Separation with kids, Breathing issues.
- 36/63 - Very religious, Multitalented, self-respect.
- 37/73 - Knowledge and success, Never harm others.
- 38/83 - Good for sales people, Good for real-estate.
- 39/93 - Show off people, Double-faced people.
- 45/54 - Very intelligent, Hospital frequency visits, Eyesight issues.
- 46/64 - Magnetic Aura, skin and piles issues.
- 47/74 - Very smart, Willpower strong.
- 58/85 - Financial issues, Money blockages.
- 67/76 - Disputes and problems in marriage or less interest in marriage.

- 68/86 - Lot of health issues.
- 79/97 - To be avoided, Blood-related issues, Joint pain and kidney issues, Ups and downs in career.
- 24/42 - Passionate to achieve something, Negative thoughts, destructive mindset, work by hook or crook.
- 26/62 - Attraction towards the opposite sex, an obstacle in study, an obstacle in life & career, health issue attracts.
- 25/52 - They always pass the mobile, they do things as per wish, as per the said things happens, success through air travel.
- 35/53 - People get success from native places, good economic condition but bad liquidity.
- 78/87 - They are good motivators, related to the healing field, Social service.
- 95/59 - Communication skill is good, straight-forward, Sharp-minded, selective in relationship.
- 54/45 - Good thought process, Don't trust easily, Active mind, Medical, Police/army.
- 51/15 - Support from father, Father Property.
- 17/71 - Solid contacts, Govt. jobs.
- 13/31 - Good Education, adviser, intelligent, good knowledge.
- 19/91 - Freedom lover, no one can restrict them.
- 43/34 - Health issue, Stubborn.
- 32/23 - Lacking response from kids, native place grows fast.
- 96/69 - Good Planner, Attraction to opposite sex.
- 62/26 - Obstacle in relationships & slow growth.
- 94/49 – Risk taker, family younger brother or sister blood-related issues/Accidents.
- 42/24 - Negative thoughts, negative mindset.
- 37/73 - Good in education or Good consultant, Good doctor.
- 38/83 - Good consultant & advisor, Good for real estate.
- 84/48 - Delay in success, struggle, litigation.
- 28/82 - Negative thought, leakage attract, good liquid cash.
- 75/57 - Success in business, success in life, growth number, dedicated, growth mindset.
- If Anyone has more than 3 Repeated numbers Called - **Freedom lover & Egoistic person.**
- Try not to repeat any number more than 4 times.
- Avoid numbers for Better results in mobile numbers –

18, 28, 29, 26, 24, 34, 36, 39, 44, 48, 43, 49, 63, 69, 81, 82, 84, 92, 94, 99.

Repetative Numbers in Mobile

11 - Aggressive and good leadership qualities.

22 - Always help others to grow in life.

33 - They will have blessings always with them.

44 - To be avoided always.

55 - Will have good communication, 55+55 create problems.

66 - Luxuries in life, relationship ups and down.

77 - Good communication, 77+77 problems in connecting people.

88 - To be avoided, lot of struggle.

99 - Good and high energy number

999/999 - Should be avoided, Aggression.

Donate in case of repeated numbers to reduce number energy

1	Feed poor People
2	Give food & pulses to Blind People
3	Medicine to needy/Patient and Poor People
4	Provided book to needful
5	Medicine to Asthama patient
6	Contibute to poor girls' Marriage
7	Food and medicine for Blinds.
8	Donation of Food in Religious Places
9	Take Blessing from Elders and seniors

Power of Rudrashya and Use as per DOB

Rudrashya is one of the Easiest and most important elements that come from Nature and work perfectly to improve and enhance number vibration. Rudrashya always being part of our Vedic Purans, and it has astrological significance also. Please find below Rudrashya wearing chart as per numerology numbers or as per Moolank and Bagyanak and how much Mukhi need to wear.

	LORD	RULLING PLANET
1-1 Mukhi	SHIVA	SUN
2-2 Mukhi	SHIV SHAKTI/SHIVA PARVATI	MOON
3-3 Mukhi	TRIDEV BRAHMA ,VISHNU, MAHESH	MARS
4-4 Mukhi	BRAHMA SWAROOP	MERCURY
5-5 Mukhi	RUDRANGA/KALYANI SWAROOP	JUPITER
6-6 Mukhi	SHIV PUTRA/KARTIKEYA	VENUS
7-7 Mukhi Lord	SAPTA RISHI	SATURN
8-8 Mukhi	LORD GANESHA	RAHU
9-9 Mukhi	NAV DURGA	KETU
10-Mukhi	DASH AVTAR	JUPITER
11-Mukhi	LORD HANUMAN	MARS
12-Mukhi	VISHNU SHIV	SUN
13-Mukhi	VISHVE-DEV	VENUS
14-Mukhi	LORD HANUMAN	SATURN
20-Mukhi	BRAHMA	MOON
21-Mukhi	LORD KUBER	VENUS
GAURI SHANKAR	SHIV PARVATI	
GANESH RUDRAKSHA	LORD GANESH	

Number There Planets, Week & Gems stones.

Celebrity Grid Analysis

MOOLANK / BAGYANK	WEEK	GEMSTONE
1-SURYA	SUNDAY	GARNET, (MANIK)
2-CHANDRA	MONDAY	AMETHYST (MOTI)
3-GURU	THURSDAY	AQUAMARINE (PILA PUKHRAJ)
4-RAHU	SUNDAY	RAHUDIAMOND (GOMED)
5-BUDH	WEDNESDAY	EMARELD (PANNA)
6-SHUKRARYA	FRIDAY	PEARL (HERA)
7-KETU	MONDAY	RUBY (LAHSUNIA)
8-SHANI	SATURDAY	PERIDOT (NELAM)
9-MANGAL	TUESDAY	BLUE TOPAZ (MUNGA)

Numbers		Colors
1		All Red shades
2		Off white
3		Yellow shades
4		Black shades
5		Green shades
6		White shades and all new colors
7		Grey shades
8		Blue and Black shade, only sky blue
9		Orange, red, maroon shades

Avoid Colors

Numbers	Colors
1	Black and Dark Blue
2	Black and Dark Blue
3	White
`4	Red
5	No
6	Yellow
7	No
8	All Red shades
9	Black, White and Dark Blue

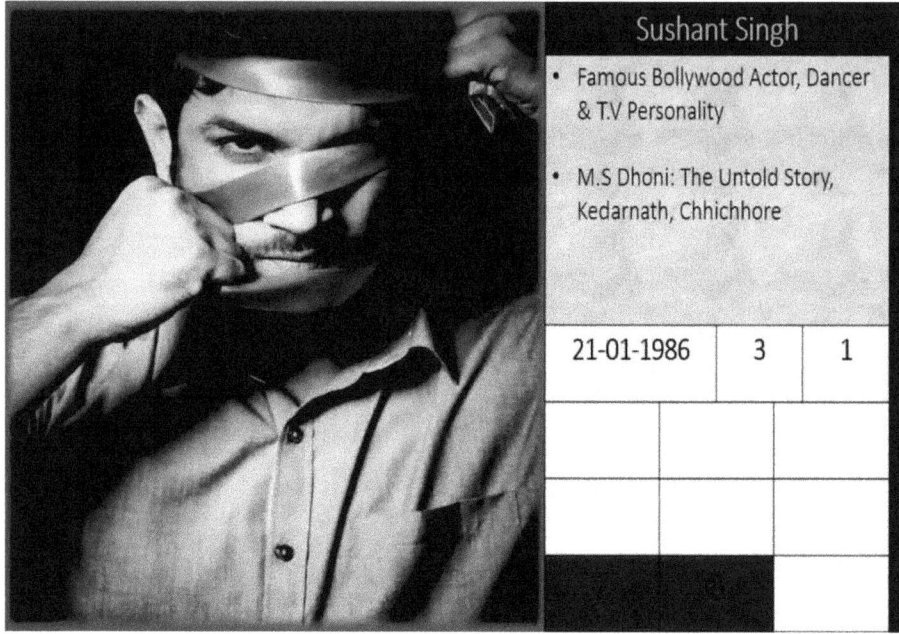

2 & 8 Lead to addiction and suicidal tendency.

2 & 8 combination lead to suicidal tendency.

Dates & Destiney

Combination of 555 makes a person money-minded and leads to cheat.

Combination of 555 leads to cheat and be money-minded.

2, 8, 4 combination gives struggle and addiction.

2 & 8 combination is negative and leads to addiction .

Combination of 22 & 4 is negative combination and leads to bankruptcy and major illness.

Cricketer and there jersey numbers.

CRICKETER NAME	JERSEY NO
VIRAT KOHLI	18
MAHENDRA SINGH DHONI	7
ROHIT SHARMA	18
SACHIN TENDULKAR	10
MOHAMMAD SHAMI	15
MOHHAMAD SIRAJ	13
RAVINDRA JADEJA	8
KULDEEP YADAV	23
KL RAHUL	1
JASPREET BUMRAH	93
WASINGTON SUNDER	5
SHREYAS AYYAR	41
SHUBHMAN GILL	77
KULDEEPN YADAV	23
HARDIK PANDYA	33

Numerology number represents various body parts and Diseases in case of disturbance.

Number	Body part	Repeated no
1	Eyes	1 no 3 times and more Anxiety, Constipation, Heart issues, UTI, Tonsils at a young age.
2	Skin, Lungs	2 no 3 times Thyroid issues, Gynec problem, Anemia, Indigestion, Asthama attack, Skin issues, Nervous breakdown, Period issues.
3	Brain	3 no more than 3 times High BP, Diabetic, Lung issues, Weak liver, Ear issues, Joindis paralysis, Allergies.
4	Sense organs	4 more than 3 times Dibetic issues, Asthama, Confussion about Diagnosis and disease.
5	Stomach	5 more than 3 Skin issues, Constipation, Insomnia, Anxiety, Sinus, Heart problem, Obesity.
6	Genitals, Sperm	6 no more than 3 times Problem with misscarriage, abortion, Gynec issues, emotional issues, UTI issues, Low sperm count.
7	Heart	7 no more than 3 times, Anxiety, overthinking, Sleeping disorder, Back pain, Shoulder pain.
8	Feet, Stomach	8 no more than 3 times Dental issues, Diabetic issues, Bones issues, UTI.
9	Blood	9 no more than 3 times Blood related issues, Sexual disorder, Stomach issues.

Celebrity numbers as per Loshu Grid

Hrithik Roshan 10/1/1974 (1/5)

4	9	2
	5	7
	111	

Strong willpower, Good communication.

Bill Gates 28/1/1955 (1/4)

	9	
	5	7
	111	

Strong willpower, Silver Rajyog, Good earth element, Intelligent, Business number.

Sunil Gavaskar 10/7/1949 (1/4)

4	9	2
	55	
8	11	

Good willpower, Intelligent, Good communication.

Aditya Chopra 21/5/1971 (3/8)

4	99	
3	5	7
8	11	

Intelligent, Struggle, Emotional .

Asaduddin Owaisi1 3/5/1969 (4/4)

4, 4	99	
3	5	
	11	6

Strong willpower, Strong-headed person, Good money, Business number.

Karan Johar 25/5/1972 (7/4)

4	9	22
	55	7
	1	

Good business number, Emotional, Intelligent.

SRK 2/11/1965 (2/7)

		2
	5	
	111	6

Sania Mirza 15/11/1986 (6/5)

	9	
	5	
8	1111	6, 6

Good willpower, Strong communication, Practical in life, Name fame, Relationship issues.

Ranveer Singh 6/7/1985 (6/9)

	9, 9	
	5	7
8	1	6, 6

Strong willpower, Practical and emotional in Life, Relationship issues.

Rahul Dravid 11/1/1973 (2/5)

	9	2
3	5	7
	1111	

Emotional, Might get cheated, Good communication, Strong will power.

Sunjay Dutt 29/7/1959 (2/6)

	999	2
	5	7
	1	

Ranbeer Kapoor 28/9/1982 (1/3)

	99	22
88	1	

Shusant Singh Rajpoot 21/1/1986 (3/1)

	9	2
3		
8	111, 1	6

Amir Khan 14/3/1965 (5/2)

4	9	2
3	5, 5	
	11	6

Intelligent, Good communication, Business-minded, Name Fame.

Deepika Padukone 5/1/1986 (5/3)

	9	
3	5, 5	
	11	6

Strong willpower, Good communication, Business-minded, Name fame.

Saif Ali Khan 16/8/1970 (7/5)

	9	
	5	7
8	11	6

Pratical in life, Strong willpower, Emotional, Name fame, Money.

Madhuri 15/5/1967 (6/7)

	9	
	55	7, 7
	11	6, 6

Beauty number, Good communication, Name and Fame, Research-oriented, Spiritual.

Kareena 21/9/1980 (3/3)

	99	2
3, 3		
8	11	

Artistic, Creative, Good communication.

Aishwarya 1/11/1973 (1/5)

	9	
3	5	7
	1111	

Emotional, Strong willpower, Good communication, Ego.

Amitabh Bacchan 11/10/1942 (2/1)

4	9	2,2
	1111	

Intelligent, Good communication, Emotional.

Sunny Deol 19/10/1957 (1/6)

	99	
	5	7
	111, 1	6

Strong willpower, Good communication, Name fame, Bit emotional.

Hema Malini 16/10/1948 (7/3)

4	9	
3		7
8	111	6

Beauty with brain number, Practical in life, Good in politics, Emotionl .

Dilip Kumar 11/12/1922 (2/1)

	9	222, 2
	1111	

Emotional, Creative, Good communication.

Jitendra 7/4/1942 (7/9)

44	9, 9	2
		7, 7
	1	

Intelligent, Spiritual, Research-oriented.

Bobby Deol 27/1/1969 (9/8)

	99, 9	2
		7
8	11	6

Practical in life, High energy, Struggle .

Kaitrina Kaif 16/7/1983 (7/8)

	9	
3		7, 7
8, 8	11	6

Beauty with brain number, Practical in life, Struggle after 35 years, Research number.

Priyanka 18/7/1982 (9/9)

	999	2
		7
88	11	

Emotional, Practical Earth element, Good communication.

Anushka Sharma 1/5/1988 (1/5)

	9	
	5, 5	
88	11, 1	

Strong willpower, Good communication, Business number.

Power of Yantras

The word Yantra has been derived from Sanskrit Language. It is composed of yam +tra = Yantra, Yam = Support, Tra = Device, Yantra means a device that supports.

Yantra helps for

- Health
- Education
- Love
- Finance
- Marriage

Yantras have power to affect your astrological planets. Hand-made yantras have more power and effect than Machine-made yantra, But certain rituals are to be followed to energize those yantras.

How to make yantra?

Mainly three things are required to make yantra

1. Bhoj Patra
2. Astgandh
3. Pomegrenate stick for writing
4. Ganga Jal.

Before making yantra, auspicious date is to be calculated or subh muhurat, like Holi, Navratri, Graghan in some cases.

Nine planets yantras

1. Surya Yantra
2. Chandra Yantra
3. Jupiter Yantra
4. Rahu Yantra
5. Budh Yantra
6. Shukra Yantra
7. Ketu Yantra
8. Shani Yantra
9. Mangal Yantra

1. Surya Yantra, Used on Sunday sun hora

6	1	8
7	5	3
2	9	4

- Use for Govt. Job
- Relationship with Father
- Fame

2. Chandra Yantra

Used on Monday Moon Hora

7	2	9
8	6	4
3	10	5

- Stress
- Depression
- Relationship with Mother
- For intuition

9. Mangal Yantra

8	3	10
9	7	5
4	11	6

- Blood-realted issues
- Surgery
- Accidents
- High BP

5. Mercury Yantra Wednesday in hora of mercury

9	4	11
10	8	6
5	12	7

- Skin disease
- Business
- Good grades
- Speech issues

3. Jupiter Yantra Thursday in Juiter hora

10	5	12
11	9	7
6	13	8

- Education
- Teaching
- Liver issues
- Consultation
- Marriage
- Good health
- Child birth

6. Shukra Yantra-Friday venus hora

11	6	13
12	10	8
7	14	9

- Luxury
- Sexual issues
- Beauty products
- Good Fortune
- Positive Energy

8. Shani Yantra-Saturday after 7 PM

12	7	14
13	11	9
8	15	10

- Arthritis
- Job
- Honour in society
- Success in Professional life
- CEO top executives

4. Rahu Yantra-Make in Saturday after 7.0 clock

13	8	15
14	12	10
9	16	11

- In case of Any addiction
- To remove unwanted obstacles
- Unstable mind
- Bacterial issues

7. Ketu-Saturday make yantra sun or Jupiter hora

14	9	16
15	13	11
10	17	12

- Spirituality
- Research
- Viral disease
- Ulcers

Making yantra at the specific hora leads to good results and chanting with mantras as per planet also effects.

Vedic Remedy

Vedic Remedy for Number 1

- Take support from Sun by giving ark to Sun from a copper vessel
- While giving ark, we must put some Sugar, Rice and Red color for extra strength
- Must put a red tika on your forehead.
- Worship Lord Shiva
- Avoid Salt on Sundays

Vedic Remedy for Number 2

- For getting Moon support, keep aquarium in the north and with the help of fishes in it; one black and one blue and 7 red or golden color fishes
- Offering water on shivling
- Always carry a green water bottle with you while traveling.
- Never Waste Water.
- Avoid Dark color Clothes
- Take Blessings from Mother, Grandmother, touch their feet.

Vedic Remedy for Number 3

- Put Saffron tilak daily
- Respect Teachers
- Use Wooden Pen
- Donate yellow Rice and sweets, and distribute them to poor people.
- Must pray on Thursday and b a n a n a (tree), put w a t e r to get support from 3.

- Avoid non-veg foods your whole life.
- Keep Yellow handkerchief
- Donate 9 pieces of frootie for marriage
- Turmeric Bath on Friday, in case of Late Marriage

Vedic Remedy for Number 4

- For remedy of Rahu, feed stray dogs daily
- Discard any non-operational electronic devices from home
- Listen to Gayatri Mantra Daily.
- Avoid non-veg and alcohol

Vedic Remedy for Number 5

- Budh, we must feed cows to get support for number 5
- Donate raw potato to cows daily will give sure shot results
- Lord Ganesha worship on Wednesday with 5 laddus.
- Offer water to Plants
- Bird Feeding is good
- Donate to Third Gender community

Vedic Remedy for Number 6

- Friday morning, prepare kheer from 2 kg milk, and donate it in the evening to poor kids
- Otherwise, donate sweets or white products (vanilla ice cream, burfi, rasgulla, white pastry) will help you get support from Venus (Shukra)
- Abroad Remedy – Donate 2 kg rice with 2 kg sugar and 2 kg milk; a total of 6 kg to nearby Gurudwara
- Take a bath in rose water

Vedic Remedy for Number 7

- Ketu by piercing your both ears
- Feeding dogs, you will get support from Ketu
- Worship Venus God and Saturn, you will get support from number 7

Vedic Remedy for Number 8

- Don't purchase any Saturn-related things on Saturday at all
- The best remedy to worship Saturn after 8 pm is just to donate Rs. 5 or Rs. 10 in the donation box to get support from Saturn.
- Feed on Saturday to disabled people.

Vedic Remedy for Number 9

- Worship Lord Hanumanji on Tuesdays and Saturdays any time; in morning, the best time is by 6 am
- Avoid Non-Veg foods your whole life
- Keep Panch Mukhi Hanumanji pic on South
- Wear red Thread on Wrist

Data base Collection of Famous Celebrity, Sportsperson, Businessmen.

Date of Birth, Collection of Famous Celebrity, Sportsperson, Businessmen.

S.No	Name	First Name	DOB	Age Today
1	Jeff Bezos	Jeff	12-01-1964	59.89
2	Elon Musk	Elon	28-06-1971	52.43
3	Bernard Arnault	Bernard	05-03-1949	74.76
4	Bill Gates	Bill	28-10-1955	68.10
5	Mark Zuckerberg	Mark	14-05-1984	39.54
6	Warren Buffett	Warren	30-08-1930	93.28
7	Larry Ellison	Larry	17-08-1944	79.31
8	Larry Page	Larry	26-03-1973	50.68
9	Sergey Brin	Sergey	21-08-1973	50.28
10	Mukesh Ambani	Mukesh	19-04-1957	66.63
11	Amancio Ortega	Amancio	28-03-1936	87.70
12	Francoise Bettencourt Meyers	Francoise	10-07-1953	70.41
13	Zhong Shanshan	Zhong	01-12-1954	69.01
14	Steve Ballmer	Steve	24-03-1956	67.70

15	Ma Huateng	Ma	29-10-1971	52.09
16	Carlos Slim Helu	Carlos	28-01-1940	83.86
17	Alice Walton	Alice	07-10-1949	74.16
18	Jim Walton	Jim	07-06-1948	75.50
19	Rob Walton	Rob	28-10-1944	79.11
20	Michael Bloomberg	Michael	14-02-1942	81.81
21	Colin Zheng Huang	Colin	16-04-1980	43.62
22	MacKenzie Scott	MacKenzie	07-04-1970	53.65
23	Daniel Gilbert	Daniel	05-11-1957	66.08
24	Gautam Adani	Gautam	24-06-1962	61.44
25	Phil Knight	Phil	24-02-1938	85.79
26	Jack Ma	Jack	10-09-1964	59.23
27	Charles Koch	Charles	01-11-1935	88.11
28	Julia Koch	Julia	12-04-1962	61.64
29	Masayoshi Son	Masayoshi	11-08-1957	66.32
30	Michael Dell	Michael	23-02-1965	58.77
31	Tadashi Yanai	Tadashi	07-02-1949	74.83
32	Francois Pinault	Francois	21-08-1936	87.30
33	David Thomson	David	12-06-1957	66.48
34	Beate Heister	Beate	05-10-1951	72.17
35	Karl Albrecht Jr.	Karl	01-01-1947	76.93
36	Wang Wei	Wang	01-10-1970	53.17
37	Miriam Adelson	Miriam	10-10-1945	78.16
38	He Xiangjian	He	05-10-1942	81.18

39	Dieter Schwarz	Dieter	24-09-1939	84.21
40	Zhang Yiming	Zhang	01-04-1983	40.66
41	Giovanni Ferrero	Giovanni	21-09-1964	59.20
42	Alain Wertheimer	Alain	28-09-1948	75.19
43	Gerard Wertheimer	Gerard	09-01-1951	72.91
44	Li Ka-shing	Li	29-07-1928	95.37
45	Qin Yinglin	Qin	01-01-1965	58.92
46	William Lei Ding	William	01-10-1971	52.17
47	Len Blavatnik	Len	14-06-1957	66.47
48	Lee Shau Kee	Lee	29-01-1928	95.87
49	Jacqueline Mars	Jacqueline	10-10-1939	84.16
50	John Mars	John	15-10-1935	88.15
51	Yang Huiyan	Yang	20-07-1981	42.36
52	Alexey Mordashov	Alexey	26-09-1965	58.18
53	Robin Zeng	Robin	01-03-1968	55.75
54	Hui Ka Yan	Hui	09-10-1958	65.15
55	Susanne Klatten	Susanne	28-04-1962	61.60
56	Vladimir Potanin	Vladimir	03-01-1961	62.92
57	Dietrich Mateschitz	Dietrich	20-05-1944	79.55
58	Pang Kang	Pang	01-01-1956	67.93
59	Klaus-Michael Kuehne	Klaus-Michael	02-06-1937	86.52
60	Vladimir Lisin	Vladimir	07-05-1956	67.58
61	Wang Xing	Wang	18-02-1979	44.78
62	German Larrea Mota Velasco	German	08-07-1941	82.42

63	Leonardo Del Vecchio	Leonardo	22-05-1935	88.55
64	Takemitsu Takizaki	Takemitsu	10-06-1945	78.49
65	Leonard Lauder	Leonard	19-03-1933	90.73
66	Thomas Peterffy	Thomas	30-09-1944	79.19
67	Vagit Alekperov	Vagit	01-09-1950	73.26
68	Leonid Mikhelson	Leonid	11-08-1955	68.32
69	Jim Simons	Jim	25-04-1938	85.62
70	Jiang Rensheng	Jiang	08-10-1953	70.16
71	Gina Rinehart	Gina	09-02-1954	69.82
72	Rupert Murdoch	Rupert	11-03-1931	92.75
73	Shiv Nadar	Shiv	14-07-1945	78.40
74	Zhang Zhidong	Zhang	01-01-1972	51.92
75	Iris Fontbona	Iris	08-01-1942	81.92
76	Lei Jun	Lei	16-12-1969	53.96
77	Zhang Yong	Zhang	01-01-1971	52.92
78	Richard Qiangdong Liu	Richard	01-01-1973	50.91
79	Gennady Timchenko	Gennady	09-11-1952	71.07
80	Stephen Schwarzman	Stephen	14-02-1947	76.81
81	Goh Cheng Liang	Goh	27-06-1927	96.46
82	Stefan Quandt	Stefan	09-05-1966	57.57
83	Li Xiting	Li	01-01-1951	72.93
84	Pierre Omidyar	Pierre	21-06-1967	56.45
85	Stefan Persson	Stefan	04-10-1947	76.18
86	Abigail Johnson	Abigail	19-12-1961	61.96

87	R. Budi Hartono	Budi	28-04-1940	83.61
88	Andrew Forrest	Andrew	18-11-1961	62.04
89	Ray Dalio	Ray	08-08-1949	74.33
90	Michael Hartono	Michael	02-10-1939	84.19
91	Li Shufu	Li	25-06-1963	60.44
92	Zhong Huijuan	Zhong	14-05-1905	118.59
93	Xu Hang	Xu	01-01-1962	61.92
94	Lui Che Woo	Lui	09-08-1929	94.34
95	Emmanuel Besnier	Emmanuel	18-09-1970	53.20
96	Laurene Powell Jobs	Laurene	06-11-1963	60.07
97	Eric Schmidt	Eric	27-04-1955	68.61
98	Sun Piaoyang	Sun	01-09-1958	65.26
99	Theo Albrecht, Jr.	Theo	28-03-1922	101.71
100	Alisher Usmanov	Alisher	09-09-1953	70.24
101	Robert Pera	Robert	10-03-1978	45.72
102	Wu Yajun	Wu	31-05-1964	59.51
103	Fan Hongwei	Fan	01-02-1967	56.83
104	Dhanin Chearavanont	Dhanin	19-04-1939	84.64
105	Peter Woo	Peter	05-09-1946	77.25
106	Chen Bang	Chen	01-09-1965	58.25
107	Andrey Melnichenko	Andrey	08-03-1972	51.73
108	Dustin Moskovitz	Dustin	22-05-1984	39.52
109	Su Hua	Su	01-01-1982	41.91
110	Donald Newhouse	Donald	01-08-1929	94.36

111	Petr Kellner	Petr	20-05-1964	59.54
112	Lee Man Tat	Lee	01-01-1930	93.94
113	Pavel Durov	Pavel	10-10-1984	39.13
114	James Ratcliffe	James	18-10-1952	71.13
115	Jorge Paulo Lemann	Jorge	16-08-1939	84.32
116	Reinhold Wuerth	Reinhold	20-04-1935	88.64
117	Charlene de Carvalho-Heineken	Charlene	30-06-1954	69.43
118	Radhakishan Damani	Radhakishan	01-01-1954	69.93
119	Wang Chuanfu	Wang	08-04-1966	57.65
120	Steve Cohen	Steve	11-06-1956	67.48
121	Ken Griffin	Ken	15-10-1968	55.13
122	Chen Zhiping	Chen	01-01-1975	48.91
123	Ernest Garcia, II	Ernest	01-05-1957	66.59
124	Uday Kotak	Uday	15-03-1959	64.72
125	Carl Icahn	Carl	16-02-1936	87.81
126	Suleiman Kerimov	Suleiman	12-03-1966	57.73
127	Thomas Frist, Jr.	Thomas	12-08-1938	85.33
128	Lukas Walton	Lukas	19-09-1986	37.19
129	Mikhail Fridman	Mikhail	21-04-1964	59.62
130	Wei Jianjun	Wei	01-01-1964	59.92
131	Zuo Hui	Zuo	01-01-1971	52.92
132	Zhou Qunfei	Zhou	01-01-1970	53.92
133	Donald Bren	Donald	11-05-1932	91.58
134	Hinduja brothers	Hinduja	28-11-1935	88.03

135	Lakshmi Mittal	Lakshmi	15-06-1950	73.48
136	Georg F.W Schaeffler	Georg	19-10-1964	59.12
137	Eric Yuan	Eric	20-02-1970	53.78
138	Wang Jianlin	Wang	24-10-1954	69.12
139	Kwong Siu-hing	Kwong	02-12-1929	94.02
140	Robin Li	Robin	17-11-1968	55.04
141	Pallonji Mistry	Pallonji	01-06-1929	94.53
142	Eduardo Saverin	Eduardo	13-03-1982	41.71
143	Roman Abramovich	Roman	24-10-1966	57.11
144	David Tepper	David	11-09-1957	66.23
145	Gong Hongjia	Gong	01-01-1965	58.92
146	Mike Cannon-Brookes	Mike	17-11-1979	44.03
147	John Menard, Jr.	John	22-01-1940	83.88
148	Seo Jung-jin	Seo	06-09-1989	34.22
149	Cheng Yixiao	Cheng	04-12-1991	31.98
150	Liang Wengen	Liang	01-12-1956	67.01
151	Scott Farquhar	Scott	01-12-1979	43.99
152	Finn Rausing	Finn	01-09-1955	68.26
153	Jorn Rausing	Jorn	12-02-1960	63.81
154	Kirsten Rausing	Kirsten	06-06-1952	71.50
155	Brian Chesky	Brian	29-08-1981	42.25
156	Joseph Lau	Joseph	21-07-1951	72.38
157	David Duffield	David	21-09-1941	82.21
158	Charoen Sirivadhanabhakdi	Charoen	02-05-1944	79.60

159	Kim Jung-ju	Kim	22-02-1968	55.78
160	Robert Ng Chee Siong	Robert	01-01-1952	71.93
161	Ng Chee Tat Philip	Philip	16-09-1958	65.22
162	Zhang Bangxin	Zhang	01-01-1980	43.91
163	Anders Holch Povlsen	Anders	04-11-1972	51.07
164	Wang Wenyin	Wang	02-03-1968	55.75
165	Tatyana Bakalchuk	Tatyana	16-10-1975	48.12
166	Michael Platt	Michael	12-12-1968	54.97
167	Huang Shilin	Huang	01-01-1967	56.92
168	Ricardo Salinas Pliego	Ricardo	19-10-1955	68.13
169	Kumar Mangalam Birla	Kumar	14-06-1967	56.47
170	Dang Yanbao	Dang	01-02-1973	50.83
171	Cyrus Poonawalla	Cyrus	01-01-1942	81.93
172	Robert Kuok	Robert	06-10-1923	100.19
173	Jack Dorsey	Jack	19-11-1976	47.03
174	Lu Zhongfang	Lu	01-12-1942	81.02
175	Ma Jianrong	Ma	01-01-1965	58.92
176	Nathan Blecharczyk	Nathan	01-01-1983	40.91
177	John Doerr	John	29-06-1951	72.44
178	Joe Gebbia	Joe	21-08-1981	42.27
179	Forrest Li	Forrest	23-05-1905	118.57
180	Gordon Moore	Gordon	03-01-1929	94.94
181	Jeff Yass	Jeff	01-01-1956	67.93
182	Bobby Murphy	Bobby	19-07-1988	35.36

183	Patrick Drahi	Patrick	20-08-1963	60.29
184	Jensen Huang	Jensen	17-02-1963	60.79
185	Alexander Otto	Alexander	07-07-1967	56.41
186	Joseph Tsai	Joseph	01-01-1964	59.92
187	Aliko Dangote	Aliko	10-04-1957	66.65
188	Marcel Herrmann Telles	Marcel	23-02-1950	73.78
189	Mikhail Prokhorov	Mikhail	03-05-1965	58.58
190	Jorge Moll Filho	Jorge	23-01-1946	77.87
191	Viktor Rashnikov	Viktor	13-10-1948	75.15
192	Harry Triguboff	Harry	03-03-1933	90.77
193	Leonid Fedun	Leonid	05-04-1956	67.67
194	Eyal Ofer	Eyal	02-06-1950	73.51
195	Evan Spiegel	Evan	04-06-1990	33.48
196	Luis Carlos Sarmiento	Luis	27-01-1933	90.87
197	Andreas Struengmann	Andreas	01-01-1950	73.93
198	Thomas Strungmann	Thomas	01-01-1950	73.93
199	Rodolphe Saadé	Rodolphe	03-03-1970	53.75
200	Dilip Shanghvi	Dilip	01-10-1955	68.18
201	Tom Love	Tom	01-10-1937	86.19
202	Wang Laisheng	Wang	01-01-1964	59.92
203	Gianluigi Aponte	Gianluigi	11-04-1960	63.65
204	Wang Laichun	Wang	01-01-1967	56.92
205	Charles Schwab	Charles	29-07-1937	86.36
206	Sunil Mittal	Sunil	23-10-1957	66.12

207	Cai Kui	Cai	01-01-1963	60.92
208	John Fredriksen	John	10-05-1944	79.58
209	German Khan	German	24-10-1961	62.11
210	Li Ge	Li	01-01-1967	56.92
211	Carl Cook	Carl	10-11-1962	61.06
212	Jan Koum	Jan	24-02-1976	47.76
213	James Dyson	James	02-05-1947	76.60
214	Iskander Makhmudov	Iskander	05-12-1963	59.99
215	Stefano Pessina	Stefano	04-06-1941	82.51
216	Quek Leng Chan	Quek	12-08-1943	80.32
217	David Geffen	David	21-02-1943	80.79
218	Jim Kennedy	Jim	01-01-1951	72.93
219	Blair Parry-Okeden	Blair	01-01-1950	73.93
220	Ding Shijia	Ding	00-01-1900	123.97
221	Sun Hongbin	Sun	01-01-1963	60.92
222	Michael Otto	Michael	12-04-1943	80.66
223	Sarath Ratanavadi	Sarath	00-01-1900	123.97
224	Xavier Niel	Xavier	25-08-1967	56.27
225	August von Finck	August	11-03-1930	93.75
226	Benu Gopal Bangur	Benu	01-01-1932	91.94
227	Thomas Kirk Kristiansen	Thomas	18-02-1979	44.78
228	Lin Bin	Lin	01-02-1968	55.83
229	Shigenobu Nagamori	Shigenobu	28-08-1944	79.28
230	Anthony von Mandl	Anthony	00-01-1900	123.97

231	Azim Premji	Azim	24-07-1945	78.37
232	Bubba Cathy	Bubba	00-01-1900	123.97
233	Nassef Sawiris	Nassef	19-01-1961	62.87
234	Andrew Beal	Andrew	29-11-1952	71.02
235	Takahisa Takahara	Takahisa	12-07-1961	62.39
236	John Malone	John	07-03-1941	82.76
237	Marijke Mars	Marijke	01-01-1965	58.92
238	Victoria Mars	Victoria	28-07-1965	58.35
239	Frederik Paulsen	Frederik	30-10-1950	73.10
240	Simon Reuben	Simon	20-05-1941	82.55
241	Alexander Abramov	Alexander	20-02-1959	64.79
242	Zhao Yan	Zhao	00-01-1900	123.97
243	Ruan Liping	Ruan	01-01-1963	60.92
244	Thierry Dassault	Thierry	26-03-1957	66.69
245	Sandra Ortega Mera	Sandra	19-07-1968	55.37
246	Rocco Commisso	Rocco	25-11-1949	74.03
247	Michael Kadoorie	Michael	19-07-1941	82.39
248	Christy Walton	Christy	08-02-1949	74.82
249	Carl Bennet	Carl	19-08-1951	72.30
250	Rahel Blocher	Rahel	18-10-1976	47.12
251	Gustaf Douglas	Gustaf	03-03-1938	85.77
252	Li Haiyan	Li	00-01-1900	123.97
253	Fredrik Lundberg	Fredrik	05-08-1951	72.34
254	Zeng Fangqin	Zeng	25-12-1965	57.94

255	Antti Herlin	Antti	14-11-1956	67.05
256	Dennis Washington	Dennis	27-07-1934	89.37
257	Margaretta Taylor	Margaretta	15-04-1942	81.65
258	Scott Duncan	Scott	01-01-1983	40.91
259	Hansjoerg Wyss	Hansjoerg	01-01-1935	88.94
260	Anil Rai Gupta	Anil	20-04-1969	54.62
261	Shyam Sunder Bhartia	Shyam	09-11-1952	71.07
262	Hari Shanker Bhartia	Hari	28-12-1956	66.93
263	Zhang Xin	Zhang	24-08-1965	58.27
264	Pan Shiyi	Pan	14-11-1963	60.05
265	Yoichi Erikawa	Yoichi	26-10-1950	73.11
266	Keiko Erikawa	Keiko	03-01-1949	74.92
267	Byju Raveendran	Byju	15-07-1981	42.37
268	Divya Gokulnath	Divya	21-04-1987	36.60
269	Philip Green	Philip	15-03-1952	71.73
270	Cristina Green	Cristina	01-08-1949	74.35
271	Ravi Ruia	Ravi	01-01-1949	74.93
272	Sachin Tendulkar	Sachin	24-04-1973	50.60
273	Mukesh Ambani	Mukesh	19-04-1957	66.63
294	Virat Kohli	Virat	05-11-1988	35.06
295	Mahendra Singh Dhoni	Mahendra	07-07-1981	42.39
296	Ekta Kapoor	Ekta	07-06-1980	43.48
297	Kareena Kapoor	Kareena	21-09-1980	43.19
298	Shahrukh Khan	Shahrukh	02-11-1965	58.08

299	Amitabh Bachchan	Amitabh	11-10-1942	81.16
300	Abhishekh Bachchan	Abhishekh	05-02-1976	47.82
301	Aishwarya Rai Bachchan	Aishwarya	01-11-1973	50.08
302	Salman Khan	Salman	27-12-1965	57.93
303	Amir Khan	Amir	14-03-1965	58.72
304	Ranbir Kapoor	Ranbir	28-09-1982	41.17
305	Ranveer Singh	Ranveer	06-07-1985	38.39
306	Kunal Khemu	Kunal	25-05-1983	40.51
307	Saif Ali Khan	Saif	16-08-1970	53.29
308	Karishma Kapoor	Karishma	25-06-1974	49.43
309	Jaya Bachchan	Jaya	09-04-1948	75.66
310	Narendra Modi	Narendra	17-09-1950	73.22
311	Uddhav Thackracy	Uddhav	27-07-1960	63.35
312	Raj Thackracy	Raj	14-06-1968	55.47
313	Aditya Thackracy	Aditya	13-06-1990	33.45
314	Alia Bhatt	Alia	15-03-1993	30.70
315	Deepika Padukone	Deepika	05-01-1986	37.89
316	Kajol	Kajol	05-08-1974	49.32
317	Ajay Devgn	Ajay	02-04-1969	54.67
318	Akshay Kumar	Akshay	09-09-1967	56.23
319	Amit Shah	Amit	22-10-1964	59.11
320	Yogi Adityanath	Yogi	05-06-1972	51.49
321	Karan Johar	Karan	25-05-1972	51.52
322	Shweta Tiwari	Shweta	04-10-1980	43.15

323	Chandan Chaudhary	Chandan	10-02-1988	35.79
324	Anupam Kher	Anupam	07-03-1955	68.75
325	Kirron Kher	Kirron	14-06-1952	71.48
326	Annu Malik	Annu	02-11-1960	63.08
327	Hema Malini	Hema	16-10-1948	75.14
328	Rekha	Rekha	10-10-1954	69.15
329	Sanjay Dutt	Sanjay	29-07-1959	64.35
330	Anil Ambani	Anil	04-06-1959	64.50
331	Sushmita Sen	Sushmita	19-11-1975	48.03
332	Milind Soman	Milind	04-11-1965	58.08
333	Mandira Bedi	Mandira	15-04-1972	51.63
334	Puneeta Kapoor	Puneeta	23-08-1973	50.27
335	Vivaan Agarwal	Vivaan	23-11-2014	8.99
336	Falguni Nayar	Falguni	19-02-1963	60.79
337	Deepinder Goyal	Deepinder	26-01-1983	40.84
338	Karan Bajaj	Karan	30-06-1979	44.42
339	Mallika Srinivasan	Mallika	19-11-1959	64.04
340	Venu Srinivasan	Venu	11-12-1952	70.98
341	Ranu Upadhyay	Ranu	16-05-1993	30.53
342	Barkha Dutt	Barkha	18-12-1971	51.95
343	Rajdeep Sardesai	Rajdeep	24-05-1965	58.53
344	Nidhi Razdan	Nidhi	11-04-1977	46.64
345	Rana Ayyub	Rana	01-05-1984	39.58
346	Sagarika Ghose	Sagarika	08-11-1964	59.07

347	Ravish Kumar	Ravish	05-12-1974	48.99
348	Arnab Goswami	Arnab	07-03-1973	50.73
349	Shekhar Gupta	Shekhar	26-08-1957	66.27
350	Prannoy Roy	Prannoy	15-10-1949	74.14
351	Barkha Singh	Barkha	03-08-1992	31.31
352	Arundhati Roy	Arundhati	24-11-1959	64.03
353	Sudhir Chaudhary	Sudhir	07-06-1974	49.48
354	Swara Bhasker	Swara	09-04-1988	35.63
355	Kartik Aryan	Kartik	22-11-1990	33.01
356	Anil Ambani	Anil	04-06-1959	64.50
357	Arvind Kejriwal	Arvind	16-08-1968	55.29
358	Gautam Adani	Gautam	24-06-1962	61.44
359	Ajit Doval	Ajit	20-01-1945	78.88
360	Ajit Thakur	Ajit	27-04-1981	42.59
361	Sharad Pawar	Sharad	12-12-1940	82.99
362	Akhilesh Yadav	Akhilesh	01-07-1973	50.42
363	Mulayam Singh Yadav	Mulayam	22-11-1939	84.05
364	Mayawati	Mayawati	15-01-1956	67.89
365	Mamta Banerjee	Mamta	05-01-1955	68.92
366	Rahul Gandhi	Rahul	19-06-1970	53.45
367	Priyanka Gandhi	Priyanka	12-01-1972	51.88
368	Laloo Prasad Yadav	Laloo	11-06-1948	75.49
369	Rajnath Singh	Rajnath	10-07-1951	72.41
370	Mukthar Ansari	Mukhtar	30-06-1963	60.43

371	Sonia Gandhi	Sonia	09-12-1946	76.99
372	Vijay Mallya	Vijay	18-12-1955	67.96
373	Kiran Mazumdar Shaw	Kiran	23-03-1953	70.70
374	Shashi Tharoor	Shashi	09-03-1956	67.74
375	Shakti Kapoor	Shakti	03-09-1952	71.25
376	Sharaddha Kapoor	Shraddha	03-03-1987	36.74
377	Disha Patani	Disha	13-06-1992	31.45
378	Kiara Advani	Kiara	31-07-1992	31.32
379	Kriti Sanon	Kriti	27-07-1990	33.33
380	Tiger Shroff	Tiger	02-03-1990	33.74
381	Jacqueline Fernandiz	Jacqueline	11-08-1985	38.30
382	Nora Fatehi	Nora	06-02-1992	31.80
383	Tara Sutaria	Tara	19-11-1995	28.02
384	Katrina Kaif	Katrina	16-07-1983	40.37
385	Ananya Pandey	Ananya	30-10-1998	25.07
386	Iliana Dcruz	Iliana	01-11-1986	37.07
387	Aditya Roy Kapoor	Aditya	16-11-1985	38.03
388	Urvashi Rautela	Urvashi	25-02-1994	29.75
390	Sara Ali Khan	Sara	12-08-1995	28.29
391	Janhvi Kapoor	Janhvi	06-03-1997	26.72
392	Arjun Kapoor	Arjun	26-06-1985	38.42
393	Malaika Arora	Malaika	23-10-1973	50.10
394	Amrita Arora	Amrita	31-01-1978	45.83
395	Mallika Sherawat	Mallika	24-10-1976	47.10

396	Poonam Pandey	Poonam	11-03-1991	32.71
397	Anurag Kashyap	Anurag	10-09-1972	51.22
398	Karan Johar	Karan	25-05-1972	51.52
399	Rajkumar Hirani	Rajkumar	20-11-1962	61.04
400	Rohit Shetty	Rohit	14-03-1974	49.72
401	Priyadarshan	Priyadarshan	30-01-1957	66.84
402	Zoya Akhtar	Zoya	14-10-1972	51.13
403	Imtiaz Ali	Imtiaz	16-06-1971	52.46
404	Vishal Bhardwaj	Vishal	04-08-1965	58.33
405	Ram Gopal Verma	Ram	07-04-1962	61.66
406	Neeraj Pandey	Neeraj	17-12-1973	49.95
407	Farhan Akhtar	Farhan	09-01-1974	49.89
408	Prakash Jha	Prakash	27-02-1952	71.77
409	Ashutosh Gowarikar	Ashutosh	15-02-1964	59.80
410	Mahesh Bhatt	Mahesh	20-09-1948	75.21
411	Pooja Shukla	Pooja	07-01-1980	43.89
412	Manoj Shukla	Manoj	20-11-1981	42.02
413	Ayan Mukherjee	Ayan	15-08-1983	40.29
414	Kabir Khan	Kabir	14-09-1968	55.21
415	SS Rajamouli	Rajamouli	10-10-1973	50.14
416	Mani Ratnam	Mani	02-06-1956	67.51
417	Anurag Basu	Anurag	08-05-1974	49.56
418	Madhur Bhandarkar	Madhura	26-08-1968	55.27
419	Aditya Chopra	Aditya	21-05-1971	52.53

420	Farah Khan	Farah	09-01-1965	58.90
421	Ali Abbas Zafar	Ali Zafar	17-01-1982	41.86
422	Tigmanshu Dhulia	Tigmanshu	03-07-1967	56.42
423	Johnny Depp	Johnny	09-06-1963	60.48
424	Joe Biden	Joe	20-11-1942	81.05
425	Emmanuel Macron	Emmanuel	21-12-1977	45.94
426	Boris Johnson	Boris	19-06-1964	59.45
427	Justin Trudeau	Justin	25-12-1971	51.93
428	Saleena Sugunan	Saleena	21-08-1978	45.27
429	Neha Kakkar	Neha	06-06-1988	35.47
430	Badshah	Badshah	19-11-1985	38.02
431	Shreya Ghosal	Shreya	12-03-1984	39.71
432	Neha Sharma	Neha	21-11-1987	36.02
433	Yo Yo Honey Singh	Yo Yo	15-03-1983	40.71
434	Jubin Nautiyal	Jubin	14-06-1989	34.45
435	Mika Singh	Mika	10-06-1977	46.47
436	Guru Randhawa	Guru	30-08-1991	32.24
437	Vishal Dadlani	Vishal	28-06-1973	50.42
438	Neha Dhupiya	Neha	27-08-1980	43.25
439	Ayushman Khurana	Aysuhman	14-09-1984	39.20
440	Tahira Kashyap	Tahira	21-06-1983	40.44
441	Rajkumar Rao	Rajkumar	31-08-1984	39.24
442	Bhumi Pednekar	Bhumi	18-07-1989	34.36
443	Yami Gautam	Yami	28-11-1988	34.99

444	Vicky Kaushal	Vicky	16-05-1988	35.53
445	Nusrat Barucha	Nursat	17-05-1985	38.53
446	Kartik Aryan	Kartik	22-11-1990	33.01
447	John Abraham	John	17-12-1972	50.95
448	Ranveer Singh	Ranveer	06-07-1985	38.39
449	Varun Dhawan	Varun	24-04-1987	36.59
450	Jitendra Kumar	Jitendra	01-09-1990	33.24
451	Neena Gupta	Neena	04-06-1959	64.50
452	Radhika Apte	Radhika	07-09-1985	38.22
453	Tabu	Tabu	04-11-1970	53.07
454	Sonam Anil Kapoor	Sonam	09-06-1985	38.47
455	Surveen Chawla	Surveen	01-08-1984	39.32
456	Nawazuddin Siddiqui	Nawazuddin	19-05-1974	49.53
457	Huma Qureshi	Huma	28-07-1986	37.33
458	Kalki Koeichlin	Kalki	10-01-1984	39.88
459	Chitragandha Singh	Chitragandha	30-08-1976	47.25
460	Vijay Raaz	Vijay	05-06-1963	60.50
461	Alu Arjun	Alu	08-04-1982	41.64
462	Rahsmika Mandana	Rashmika	05-04-1996	27.64
463	Samantha Prabhu	Samantha	28-04-1987	36.58
464	Prakash Raj	Prakash	26-03-1965	58.69
465	Nagaarjuna Rao	Nagaarjuna	29-08-1959	64.27
466	Prabhas	Prabhas	23-10-1979	44.10
467	Nagma	Nagma	25-12-1974	48.93

468	Sourav Ganguly	Sourav	08-07-1972	51.40
469	Rahul Dravid	Rahul	11-01-1973	50.88
470	Virendra Sehwag	Veeru	20-10-1978	45.11
471	VVS Laxman	VVS	01-11-1974	49.08
472	Anil Kumble	Anil	17-10-1970	53.12
473	Sunil Gavaskar	Sunil	10-07-1949	74.41
474	Kapil Deo	Kapil	06-01-1959	64.91
475	Rohit Sharma	Rohit Sharma	30-04-1987	36.58
476	Gautam Gambhir	Gautam	14-10-1981	42.12
477	Ravi Shashtri	Ravi	27-05-1962	61.52
478	Rishabh Pant	Rishabh	04-10-1997	26.14
479	Shreyas Iyer	Shreyas	06-12-1994	28.97
480	Ravindra Jadeja	Ravindra	06-12-1988	34.97
481	KL Rahul	Rahul	18-04-1992	31.61
482	Hardik Pandya	Hardik	11-10-1993	30.12
483	Mohammed Shami	Shami	03-09-1990	33.23
484	Yuzvendra Chahal	Yuzvendra	23-07-1990	33.35
485	Bhuvneshwar Kumar	Bhuvi	05-02-1990	33.81
486	Donald Trump	Donald	14-06-1946	77.48
487	Xi Jinping	Xi	15-06-1953	70.47
488	Aang San su Kyi	Aang	19-06-1945	78.47
489	Mithun Chakraborty	Mithun	16-06-1950	73.47
490	Angelina Jolie	Angelina	04-06-1975	48.49
491	Nicole Kidman	Nicole	20-06-1967	56.45

492	Liam Neeson	Liam	07-06-1952	71.50
493	Yogi Adityanath	Yogi	05-06-1972	51.49
494	Joko Widodo	Joko	21-06-1961	62.45
495	Tamim bin Hamad al Thani	Tamim	03-06-1980	43.49
496	Kiran Bedi	Kiran	09-06-1949	74.49
497	Laloo Prasad Yadav	Laloo	11-06-1948	75.49
498	Piyush Goel	Piyush	13-06-1964	59.47
500	Bobby Jindal	Bobby	10-06-1971	52.48
501	Akbaruddin Owaisi	Akbaruddin	14-06-1970	53.47
502	Kironn Kher	Kironn	14-06-1955	68.48
503	Mikhail Khodorovasky	Mikhail	26-06-1963	60.44
504	Mateusz Morawiecki	Mateusz	20-06-1968	55.45
505	Supriya Sule	Supriya	30-06-1969	54.42
506	Sanath Jayasuriya	Sanath	30-06-1969	54.42
507	Subrata Roy	Subrata	10-06-1948	75.49
508	Narendra Singh Tomar	Narendra	12-06-1957	66.48
509	Shah Mehmood Qureshi	Mehmood	22-06-1956	67.45
510	Nikol Pashinyan	Nikol	01-06-1975	48.50
511	Fazal ur Rehman	Fazal	19-06-1953	70.46
512	Prashant Bhushan	Prashant	23-06-1956	67.45
513	Yousaf Raza Gillani	Yousuf	09-06-1952	71.49
514	Justin Bieber	Justin	01-03-1994	29.74
515	Selena Gomez	Selena	22-07-1992	31.35
516	Miley Cyrus	Miley	23-11-1992	31.01

517	Liam Hemsworth	Liam	13-01-1990	33.87
518	Kim Kardarshian	Kim	21-10-1980	43.10
519	Taylor Swift	Taylor	13-12-1989	33.95
520	Tony Abott	Tony	04-11-1957	66.08
521	Kim Jong Un	Kim	08-01-1983	40.89
522	Angela Merkel	Angela	17-07-1954	69.39
523	Sundar Pichai	Sundar	10-06-1972	51.47
524	Kate Upton	Kate	10-06-1992	31.46
525	Anjana Om Kashyap	Anjana	12-06-1975	48.47
526	Javed Miandad	Javed	12-06-1957	66.48
527	Carla Abellana	Carla	12-06-1986	37.46
528	Balchandra Kadam	Balchandra	12-06-1992	31.45
529	Imran Khan	Imran	05-10-1952	71.17
530	Pervez Musharraf	Pervez	11-08-1943	80.33
531	Sonakshi Sinha	Sonakshi	02-06-1987	36.49
532	Mahua Moitra	Mahua	12-10-1974	49.13
533	Nupur Sharma	Nupur	23-04-1985	38.60
534	Manisha Koirala	Manisha	16-08-1970	53.29
535	Saif Ali Khan	Saif	16-08-1970	53.29
536	Sinzo Abe	Sinzo	21-09-1953	70.21
537	Aryan Khan	Aryan	13-11-1997	26.03
538	Palki Sharma Upadhyay	Palki	29-05-1982	41.50
539	Anshul Jaiswal	Anshul	05-05-1984	39.56
540	Bill Clinton	Bill	19-08-1946	77.30

541	Bhoomi Pednekar	Bhoomi	18-07-1989	34.36
542	Lalit Modi	Lalit	29-11-1965	58.01
543	Leonardo DiCaprio	Leonardo	11-11-1974	49.05
544	Dwayne Johnson	Dwayne	02-05-1972	51.58
545	Jennifer Aniston	Jennifer	11-02-1969	54.80
546	Brad Pitt	Brad	18-12-1963	59.96
547	George Clooney	George	06-05-1961	62.58
548	Tom Hanks	Tom	09-07-1956	67.41
549	Sandra Bullock	Sandra	26-07-1964	59.35
550	Robert Downey Jr.	Robert	04-04-1965	58.66
551	Julia Roberts	Julia	28-10-1967	56.10
552	Mel Gibson	Mel	03-01-1956	67.92
553	Bruce Willis	Bruce	19-03-1955	68.72
554	Oprah Winfrey	Oprah	29-01-1954	69.85
555	David Beckham	David	02-05-1975	48.58
556	Will Smith	Will	25-09-1968	55.18
557	Jennifer Lopez	Jennifer	24-07-1969	54.36
558	Tiger Woods	Tiger	30-12-1975	47.92
559	Ellen DeGeneres	Ellen	26-01-1958	65.85
560	Cristiano Ronaldo	Cristiano	05-05-1985	38.56
561	Emma Watson	Emma	15-04-1990	33.62
562	Simon Cowell	Simon	07-10-1959	64.16
563	Scarlett Johnson	Scarlett	22-11-1984	39.01
564	Jim Carrey	Jim	17-01-1962	61.88

565	Chris Hemsworth	Chris	11-08-1983	40.30
566	Lionel Messi	Lionel	24-06-1987	36.43
567	Neymar Jr.	Neymar	05-02-1992	31.81
568	Roger Federer	Roger	08-08-1981	42.31
569	Novak DjoKovic	Novak	22-05-1987	36.52
570	Andy Murray	Andy	15-05-1987	36.54
571	Serena Williams	Serena	26-09-1981	42.17
572	Andre Agassi	Andre	29-04-1970	53.59
573	Sania Mirza	Sania	15-11-1986	37.03
574	Rohan Bopanna	Rohan	04-03-1980	43.74
575	Saina Nehwal	Saina	17-03-1990	33.70
576	Leander Paes	Leander	17-06-1973	50.45
577	Mahesh Bhupathi	Mahesh	07-06-1974	49.48
578	Martina Hingis	Martina	30-09-1980	43.16
579	PV Sindhu	PV	05-07-1995	28.39
580	Maria Sharapova	Maria	19-04-1987	36.61
581	Rafael Nadal	Rafael	03-06-1986	37.48
582	Ankita Raina	Ankita	11-01-1993	30.87
583	Mary Kom	Mary	24-11-1982	41.01
584	Ariana Grande	Ariana	26-06-1993	30.42
585	Selena Gomez	Selena	22-07-1992	31.35
586	Taylor Swift	Taylor	13-12-1989	33.95
587	Chris Evans	Chris	13-06-1981	42.46
588	Rihanna	Rihanna	20-02-1988	35.77

589	Jennifer Stone	Jennifer	12-02-1993	30.78
590	Britney Spears	Britney	02-12-1981	41.99
591	Kylie Jenner	Kylie	10-08-1997	26.29
592	Beyonce	Beyonce	04-09-1981	42.23
593	Lady Gaga	Lady	28-03-1986	37.67
594	Barak Obama	Barak	04-08-1961	62.33
595	Hillary Clinton	Hillary	26-10-1947	76.12
596	Melania Trump	Melania	26-04-1970	53.60
597	Abdul Hamid	Abdul	01-01-1944	79.93
598	Sheikh Hasina	Hasina	28-09-1947	76.19
599	Babar Azam	Babar	15-10-1994	29.11
600	Fakhar Zaman	Fakhar	10-04-1990	33.63
601	Shoaib Malik	Shoaib	01-02-1982	41.82
602	Sarfaraz Ahmed	Sarfaraz	22-05-1987	36.52
603	Joe Root	Joe	30-12-1990	32.91
604	KL Rahul	Rahul	18-04-1992	31.61
605	Kane Williamson	Kane	08-08-1990	33.30
606	Mohammad Amir	Amir	13-04-1992	31.62
607	Steve Smith	Steve	02-06-1989	34.48
608	David Warner	David	27-10-1986	37.08
609	Pat Cummins	Pat	08-05-1993	30.55
610	Aaron Finch	Aaron	17-11-1986	37.03
611	Glenn Maxwell	Glenn	14-10-1988	35.12
612	Mitchell Starc	Mitchell	30-01-1990	33.82

613	Ben Stokes	Ben	04-06-1991	32.48
614	Ricky Ponting	Ricky	19-12-1974	48.95
615	Tim Paine	Tim	08-12-1984	38.97
616	Jos Buttler	Jos	08-09-1990	33.22
617	AB Dev Velliers	AB	17-02-1984	39.78
618	Jonny Bairstaw	Jonny	26-09-1989	34.17
619	Jofra Archer	Jofra	01-04-1995	28.65
620	Brian Lara	Brian	02-05-1969	54.58
621	Chris Gayle	Chris	21-09-1979	44.19
622	Kieron Pollard	Kieron	12-05-1987	36.55
623	Dwayne Bravo	Dwayne	07-10-1983	40.14
624	Andre Russel	Andre	29-04-1988	35.58
625	Shimron Hetmyer	Shimron	26-12-1996	26.91
626	Yuzvendra Chahal	Yuzvendra	23-07-1990	33.35
627	Hardik Pandya	Hardik	11-10-1993	30.12
628	Yuzvendra Chahal	Yuzvendra	23-07-1990	33.35
629	Hardik Pandya	Hardik	11-10-1993	30.12
630	Tesla	Tesla	01-07-2003	20.40
631	SpaceEx	SpaceEx	14-03-2002	21.70
632	Droupadi Murmu	Droupadi	20-06-1958	65.46
633	Volodymyr Zelenskyy	Volodymyr	25-01-1978	45.84
634	Sonu Sood	Sonu	30-07-1973	50.34

My final message to all my readers I have kept the book in a simplest forms that it is to be read by any one apart from any age group and start using power of numbers, All the concepts are given are based upon various teachers and my personal observation still IF any concept is not up to the mark I felt very sorry and hope to give you benefit of buying these book and sincere thanks to all readers to give me a chance to share my opinion about numerology.

Hope and pray to god for your well being and growth.

For all my all my readers send a copy of my book with pic on my no and with review get intial grid reading free with tarot card reading and Free intial Signature analysis.

My sincere Regards

By Astro Abhijeet

My other interest and knowledge Since I am born on 3/12/1982 with driver no 3 and conductor no 8, My keen interest in learning new modalities of occult science. Iam certified Signature anlyst and Tarrot card reader, I am Dowsing healer also and also trained many student in dowsing rods healing, It is best used to scanned energy positive or negative, Knowing various doshas like Bandhan dosh, Kalsarp dosh, Black magic, TO know power of Rudrskhya, Gem stone it is very effective. Soon My my new book "SPIRITUAL BUTTERFLIES" is on the floor.

Follow me on my Face book PAGE-ASTRO ABHIJEET

INSTARAM PAGE – ASTRO ABHIJEET

YOUTUBE PAGE – ASTRO ABHIJEET

www.astroabhijeet.com

www.ingramcontent.com/pod-product-compliance
Lightning Source LLC
LaVergne TN
LVHW070531070526
838199LV00075B/6752